GOODMAN'S FIVE-STAR STORIES

# CH!LLS

## 12 Chilling Tales and Exciting Adventures
### With Exercises to Help You LEARN

*By Burton Goodman*

JAMESTOWN PUBLISHERS

*a division of* NTC/CONTEMPORARY PUBLISHING GROUP
Lincolnwood, Illinois USA

## TITLES IN THE SERIES

| | | | |
|---|---|---|---|
| Adventures | Level B | After Shocks | Level E |
| More Adventures | Level B | Sudden Twists | Level F |
| Chills | Level C | More Twists | Level F |
| More Chills | Level C | Encounters | Level G |
| Surprises | Level D | More Encounters | Level G |
| More Surprises | Level D | Conflicts | Level H |
| Shocks | Level E | More Conflicts | Level H |

## Chills

Editorial Director: Cynthia Krejcsi
Executive Editor: Marilyn Cunningham
Project Editor: Christine Lund Orciuch
Production: Thomas D. Scharf
Cover design: Kristy Sheldon
Cover illustration: Bob Eggleton

ISBN: 0-89061-858-5

Published by Jamestown Publishers,
a division of NTC/Contemporary Publishing Group, Inc.,
4255 West Touhy Avenue,
Lincolnwood (Chicago), Illinois 60712-1975 U.S.A.
© 1997 by Burton Goodman

00 01 02 03 04 QM 14 13 12 11 10 9 8 7 6

# Contents

To the Student . . . . . . . . . . . . . . . . . . . . . . . . . . . . . . . . . . . 1

**The Short Story—Important Literary Words** . . . . . . . . . . . . . . 5

**1. The Old House** *by W. W. Jacobs* . . . . . . . . . . . . . . . . . . . 6

**2. Uneasy Homecoming** *by Will F. Jenkins* . . . . . . . . . . . . . 18

**3. Mean Rocky** *by George Shea* . . . . . . . . . . . . . . . . . . . . 28

**4. The Three Brothers and the Treasure** *by José Maria Eça de Queiroz* . . 36

**5. His Best Time** *by Elizabeth Van Steenwyk* . . . . . . . . . . . . 48

**6. The Attic Door** *by Judith Bauer Stamper* . . . . . . . . . . . . . 58

**7. The Cricket** *retold by Joe Hayes* . . . . . . . . . . . . . . . . . . 70

**8. The Ghost of Wan Li Road** *by Kara Dalkey* . . . . . . . . . . . 82

**9. The Family** *based on a story by Anton Chekhov* . . . . . . . . . 94

**10. A Helping Hand** *by Janet Ritchie* . . . . . . . . . . . . . . . . . 104

**11. The Shop** *by H. G. Wells* . . . . . . . . . . . . . . . . . . . . . . 114

**12. It's So Wonderful Here** *by Bill Pronzini* . . . . . . . . . . . . . 126

**Acknowledgments** . . . . . . . . . . . . . . . . . . . . . . . . . . . . . 137

**Progress Chart** . . . . . . . . . . . . . . . . . . . . . . . . . . . . . . . 138

**Progress Graph** . . . . . . . . . . . . . . . . . . . . . . . . . . . . . . 139

# To the Student

There are 12 very exciting short stories in *Chills*. I have picked these stories because I like them so much. I believe that you will like them too.

These stories will give you hours of reading fun. And you will enjoy doing the exercises that follow each story.

The exercises will help you LEARN important reading and literature skills:

LOOKING FOR FACTS IN THE STORY

EXAMINING VOCABULARY WORDS

ADDING WORDS TO A PARAGRAPH

READING BETWEEN THE LINES

NOTING STORY ELEMENTS

LOOKING FOR FACTS IN THE STORY helps you find key facts in a story. Sometimes these facts are called *details*.

EXAMINING VOCABULARY WORDS helps you strengthen your vocabulary skills. Often, you can figure out the meaning of a new word by looking at the words around the unfamiliar word. When you do this, you are using *context clues*. In each story, the vocabulary words are printed in **boldface type.** If you wish, look back at these words when you answer the vocabulary questions.

ADDING WORDS TO A PARAGRAPH helps you strengthen your reading *and* your vocabulary skills. This part uses fill-in, or cloze, exercises.

READING BETWEEN THE LINES helps you sharpen your *critical thinking* skills. You will have to think about what happened in the story, and then figure out the answers.

NOTING STORY ELEMENTS helps you understand some important elements of literature. Some story elements are *plot, character, setting,* and *mood.* On page 5 you will find the meaning of these and other words. If you wish, look back at those meanings when you answer the questions.

Another part, **THINKING MORE ABOUT THE STORY,** gives you a chance to think, talk, and write about the story.

Here is the way to do the exercises:

- There are four questions for each of the LEARN exercises above.

- Do all the exercises.

- Check your answers with your teacher.

- Use the scoring chart at the end of each exercise to figure out your score for that exercise. Give yourself 5 points for each correct answer. (Since there are four questions, you can get up to 20 points for each exercise.)

- Use the LEARN scoring chart at the end of the exercises to figure your total score. If you get all the questions right, your score will be 100.

- Keep track of how well you do by writing in your Score Total on the **Progress Chart** on page 138. Then write your score on the **Progress Graph** on page 139. By looking at the Progress Graph, you can see how much you improve.

I know that you will enjoy reading the stories in this book. And the exercises that follow the stories will help you LEARN some very important skills.

Now . . . get ready for some *Chills.*

Burton Goodman

# The Short Story—Important Literary Words

**Characterization:** how a writer shows what a character is like. The way a character acts, speaks, thinks, and looks *characterizes* that person.

**Main Character:** the person the story is mostly about.

**Mood:** the feeling that the writer brings about, or creates. For example, the *mood* of a story might be happy or sad.

**Plot:** the actions or events that take place in a story. The first thing that happens in a story is the first action or event that takes place in the *plot.*

**Setting:** where and when the story takes place. The *setting* is the time and the place of the action in a story.

**Theme:** the main idea of the story.

# 1

# *The Old House*

by W. W. Jacobs

A haunted house?" said Jack Barnes. He smiled. "There is no such thing as a haunted house."

Jack was talking to Lester, Fred, and William. The men were eating lunch at the Mayfair Inn. All four had spent the morning hiking. Every summer they met to hike. They always hiked for two weeks in the countryside.

Lester said, "That house on the hill *is* haunted."

"There is no such thing as a haunted house," Jack said.

"But people have died in that house," said Fred.

"Of course people have died in the house," said Jack. "People have died in lots of houses."

"How can you explain the noises?" asked William. "The people in the village say they hear strange noises coming from the house."

"Bah!" said Jack. He bit into his sandwich. "Just the wind in the chimney. Just mice in the attic."

Lester suddenly said, "I'll bet you twenty dollars you won't spend the night there alone! I bet you're afraid to spend the night there alone!"

"I'll bet you twenty dollars too!" added William.

"Well," Jack said softly. "I don't believe in ghosts. Still, I wouldn't want to spend the night there alone."

"Why not?" asked Lester. "Afraid of the wind in the chimney?"

"Afraid of the mice in the attic?" said William.

"No," Jack said. "I just wouldn't like to spend a night in that house alone."

"Suppose we *all* go?" William said suddenly. "We could leave after dinner. We'd get to the house around eleven at night. We've been hiking for a week without an adventure. That will be something new, at least."

"I don't know," said Jack.

"Afraid?" asked Lester.

"All right, then," said Jack. "We'll leave after dinner."


There was little light from the moon, and the sky was cloudy. The road was dark. The men **stumbled** often on the rocky path.

"The house should be somewhere just ahead," said William.

"No. It's still farther on," said Fred.

"That old house will be dark at night," said Jack. "You didn't forget to bring candles, did you, Lester?"

"I brought two," said Lester. "That was all that they had at the inn."

The men walked on for a while without talking. Then they saw the old house. It was on top of a hill. Tall, thick **shrubs** grew around the house. There was a graveyard nearby. The men looked at it, then walked very quickly around the graveyard.

"There are windows in the back," said Lester. "We can get in the house that way."

"No. Let's try the front door," said William. He stepped forward. Then he banged his fists loudly against the door.

"Stop playing games," said Jack. "You know that there's no one inside the house."

"I guess all the ghosts are asleep," said William. He laughed. "But don't worry. I'll wake them up." He banged on the door again. Then he suddenly cried out as the door slowly opened.

"Why, it was open all the time," he said, surprised.

"I don't believe it was open," said Fred. He looked worried.

"It *must* have been," said Lester. "I've got a candle. Who has a match?"

"I do," said Jack. He struck a match and lighted the candle. Then Lester led the way into the house.

"Somebody shut the door," said William. "There's a bit of a breeze. The candle will go out."

"It *is* shut," said Fred, looking behind him.

"Who shut it?" asked William. "Who came in last?"

"I did," said Jack. "I don't remember shutting the door. But it is possible that I did."

Lester moved slowly. He held the candle in front of him. The other men followed. They looked all around.

Shadows danced on the walls. Shadows jumped around the corners. Shadows and darkness **surrounded** the men.

"Look," said Lester. "There's a staircase ahead." Slowly they started to climb up the steps.

"Be careful!" warned Lester when they got to the top. "Part of the railing is missing up here." He held out the candle. The men saw that part of the railing was gone. They looked through the open space to the floor down below.

"Perhaps someone slipped and fell through the railing," said Lester.

"Or perhaps he was *pushed* over the side," William whispered.

"Don't talk that way!" cried Fred. "This house is scary enough without talking that way!"

Lester opened the door to a small, square room. "Let's rest here," he said.

He set down the candle.

The men seated themselves on the floor. Fred opened the bag. He took out a bottle of water and four paper cups.

"Wait! Do you hear that!" cried Jack.

"What is it?" said Fred. "Do you hear someone coming?"

Jack said, "I don't believe in ghosts. But I thought I heard a door open below. I thought I heard footsteps outside on the stairs."

"Well, well, well," Lester said. "You don't believe in—"

He suddenly stopped as the light went out. The men jumped to their feet. They stood there in the darkness.

"It's only the candle," said William. "The candle went out."

Jack struck a match. He lighted the candle again.

"Quiet!" said Fred. "I thought—I thought I heard someone talking outside."

Jack said, "I'm getting tired of this game. I keep hearing things too. It's just my imagination, I know. But this place sure is creepy."

Jack got up. He walked to the half-closed door and listened.

"Afraid?" said Lester. "Afraid to go outside?"

Jack sat down. "There can't *really* be anything out there," he said. "But we *did* hear noises. What do you think, Fred?"

Fred did not answer.

"Why, he's asleep," William said. "Wake up, Fred!" shouted William. "*Wake up,* I say!"

But Fred did not move. He sat with his back against the wall. His head was bowed. His eyes were tightly shut.

Lester turned to the others. "He sleeps like the dead," he said.

"Nonsense!" said Jack. "He's just tired from hiking. He needs some fresh air. Let's carry him outside. Lester, you take his legs. I'll take his arms. William, you can hold the candle and lead the way. Okay, Lester. You take his legs. *Lester!—Lester!*"

But it was too late. Lester's face was buried in his arms. He had rolled over on the floor. He was fast asleep.

"We must get out of here *now!*" said William. His voice was shaking.

"But we can't leave them here!" said Jack.

"We must!" urged William. "Quickly! Come!"

Jack turned toward the door. Suddenly he heard a noise. William had slipped to the floor and was fast asleep.

Jack did not move. By the light of the candle he saw the three sleeping men. Jack listened. He thought he heard a noise outside.

"Who's there?" he shouted.

The noise suddenly stopped.

Jack walked to the door and stepped out into the hall. He no longer felt afraid.

"Come on!" he yelled. "Come on! Show your faces!"

Jack walked down the hall.

As soon as Jack was gone, William jumped to his feet. "That was a good trick," he said to Lester and Fred. "Jack really thought we were asleep. Let's go after him now."

There was no answer from Lester and Fred. William said, "Stop fooling around! Stop making believe that you're asleep! *Lester! Fred!* Do you hear! Do you hear!"

The men did not answer. "All right," said William. "Play your games!"

William stood for a few seconds and watched the men. The silence was terrible. He could not even hear them breathe. He grabbed the candle. Then he went out into the hall.

He heard footsteps coming up the stairs. The candle shook in his hand. The footsteps stopped. William walked a little way along the hall. Then he heard the footsteps again. They were running down the stairs.

William walked to the railing. He saw the part that had been torn away. He looked down into the blackness below. Then, he slowly and **cautiously** made his way down the stairs.

"Jack!" he called. "Are you there, Jack?"

Shaking with fright, he reached the bottom of the steps. He looked, with fear, into empty rooms. Then, suddenly, he heard footsteps behind him.

He turned and followed them slowly. By the light of the candle he saw a door closing. He walked to the door. He threw it open.

A sudden breeze from inside blew out the candle!

He stood there, shocked.

"Jack!" he called out. "It's me! It's William!"

There was no answer. He stood staring into darkness. But he had the feeling that someone was watching him.

Then he heard the footsteps again. They were climbing up the stairs.

Slowly he moved toward the stairs. He could see better in the darkness now. He saw the stairs. He began to climb them.

He reached the top of the steps. He saw a figure disappear in the shadows. William began to follow the sound of the footsteps.

"Jack!" he called.

Something moved in the darkness. It was coming closer to him.

"Jack?" yelled William. "Is that *you*—Jack?"

The figure did not answer. Closer and closer it came. William turned. He began to run down the hall. If he could get to the staircase! If he could reach the front door!

William ran faster. But something was running after him! It was right behind him! William jumped to the side to let it pass. Then he suddenly seemed to fall off the earth and out into space.

Lester awoke in the morning. He saw sunlight shining into the room. Fred was just getting up.

"Where are the others?" asked Lester.

"Gone, I guess," said Fred. "We must have been asleep."

Lester got up. He dusted off his clothes. Then he walked out into the hall. Fred followed. Their noise woke up a figure who had been lying asleep in the hall. It was Jack.

"Why, I've been asleep," he said, surprised. Jack looked around. "Where's William?" he asked. Nobody knew.

"That's funny. I don't remember coming out here into the hall."

"Bad place to take a nap," said Lester. He pointed to the part of the railing that was gone. "Another few feet and you might have gone over the edge."

Lester walked over to the railing and looked down. He cried out. The other men came near. All three stood staring down at the dead man below.

## LOOKING FOR FACTS IN THE STORY.

How well can you find facts in a story? Put an *x* in the box next to the right answer.

1. Every summer the men hiked for
   - ❑ a. two weeks.
   - ❑ b. a month.
   - ❑ c. two months.

2. Fred opened a bag and took out
   - ❑ a. a sandwich.
   - ❑ b. a bottle of water.
   - ❑ c. some candles.

3. Jack fell asleep
   - ❑ a. on the stairs.
   - ❑ b. in the kitchen.
   - ❑ c. in the hall.

4. At the end of the story, the men saw
   - ❑ a. a ghost.
   - ❑ b. some mice.
   - ❑ c. a dead man.

## EXAMINING VOCABULARY WORDS.

Here are four vocabulary questions. Put an *x* in the box next to the right answer. The vocabulary words are printed in **boldface** in the story. You may look back at the words before you answer the questions.

1. Since it was dark, the men stumbled on the path. The word *stumbled* means
   - ❑ a. laughed.
   - ❑ b. jumped.
   - ❑ c. fell.

2. Tall, thick shrubs grew around the house. What are *shrubs*?
   - ❑ a. bushes
   - ❑ b. flowers
   - ❑ c. gates

3. Shadows surrounded the men. The word *surrounded* means
   - ❑ a. attacked.
   - ❑ b. helped.
   - ❑ c. were around.

4. He slowly and cautiously walked down the steps. The word *cautiously* means
   - ❑ a. happily.
   - ❑ b. carefully.
   - ❑ c. suddenly.

x 5 =

NUMBER CORRECT     YOUR SCORE

x 5 =

NUMBER CORRECT     YOUR SCORE

# A
**ADDING WORDS TO A PARAGRAPH.** Complete the paragraph below. Fill in each blank with one of the words in the box. Each word appears in the story. There are five words and four blanks, so one word in the box will not be used.

Every year thousands of

_____ go on hiking
　　　　　1

trips. Some trips last for several

_____ or even
　　　　2

months. But it is also

_____ to hike for
　　　　3

just an hour or two. If you enjoy

walking and fresh air, you will

probably like _____ .
　　　　　　　　　4

| weeks | people | dark |
|-------|--------|------|
| possible | hiking | |

# R
**READING BETWEEN THE LINES.** These questions will help you think critically. You will have to think about what happened in the story, and then figure out the answers. Put an *x* in the box next to the right answer.

1. At the end of the story, William
   - ❑ a. died.
   - ❑ b. joked with the other men.
   - ❑ c. went home.

2. We may infer (figure out) that William
   - ❑ a. was shot.
   - ❑ b. got into a fight with Jack.
   - ❑ c. fell through the railing.

3. Which was most frightening?
   - ❑ a. The house was on top of a hill.
   - ❑ b. The house was very old.
   - ❑ c. The front door seemed to open and close by itself.

4. The writer tries to make you think that
   - ❑ a. the men are alone in the house.
   - ❑ b. there may be ghosts in the house.
   - ❑ c. Fred is the smartest man.

[____] x **5** = [____]

**NUMBER CORRECT**　　　**YOUR SCORE**

[____] x **5** = [____]

**NUMBER CORRECT**　　　**YOUR SCORE**

# NOTING STORY ELEMENTS.

Some story elements are **plot, character, setting,** and **mood.** Put an *x* in the box next to the right answer.

1. What happened first in the *plot*?
   - ❏ a. William tried to wake up Fred.
   - ❏ b. The men walked along a dark road.
   - ❏ c. A breeze blew out the candles.

2. Which sentence best *characterizes* Jack?
   - ❏ a. He thought that most houses were haunted.
   - ❏ b. He tried to trick the other men.
   - ❏ c. He said he didn't believe in ghosts.

3. What is the *setting* of the story?
   - ❏ a. the Mayfair Inn
   - ❏ b. an old, dark house
   - ❏ c. a country road

4. Which word tells the *mood* of the story?
   - ❏ a. scary
   - ❏ b. funny
   - ❏ c. happy

[ ] x **5** = [ ]

NUMBER        YOUR
CORRECT       SCORE

**THINKING MORE ABOUT THE STORY.** Your teacher might want you to write your answers.

- ◆ Do you think that the men were alone in the house? Why?
- ◆ How can you explain the noises that the men heard?
- ◆ Suppose that William had stopped running down the hall. How do you think the story would have ended?

Use the boxes below to total your scores for the exercises. Then write your score on pages 138 and 139.

[ ] **L** OOKING FOR FACTS IN THE STORY
+
[ ] **E** XAMINING VOCABULARY WORDS
+
[ ] **A** DDING WORDS TO A PARAGRAPH
+
[ ] **R** EADING BETWEEN THE LINES
+
[ ] **N** OTING STORY ELEMENTS
▼
[ ] **SCORE TOTAL:** Story 1

17

# 2

# *Uneasy Homecoming*

by Will F. Jenkins

Connie was glad to be going home. She and her husband, Tom, had enjoyed their trip. They had a wonderful time. The weather had been great. They had to return a day early, but she was glad to be back.

The taxi stopped in front of her house. It was easy to find. It was the only one on that side of the lake.

Connie paid the driver. He took out her suitcases and put them inside the door. Then he left. She heard the sound of the car as it moved away.

Connie walked across the room. She looked out the window. The sun was beginning to go down. She could see the houses on the other side of the lake. She had friends who lived over there. She would call some of them later to find out if anything was new.

The house looked neat, and it was good to be home. Tom would be back around midnight. He had stayed to take care of some last minute business.

Connie opened the front door to let in some fresh air. It was quiet outside the house. Birds usually sang during the day. But now it was getting dark. And there were no neighbors to make any sounds.

Connie went outside. She was eager to see her garden. The flowers looked beautiful in the dim light. She loved the smells of summer evenings.

Connie looked across the lake. She saw the lights in the houses there. Suddenly, Connie felt uneasy. She did not know why. But she felt that something was wrong.

Connie walked quickly toward the house. She heard her footsteps on the path. Leaves brushed against her feet. She told herself, "Don't rush. There is no need for you to hurry."

Connie came to the front of her house. She went inside and locked the door. "Why am I so nervous?" she asked herself. She answered, "The trip was long. You're tired. It's dark. And you're alone."

Connie turned on the light in the hall. She turned on the lights in the other rooms. "Should I look upstairs?" she wondered. "No," she said, angry with herself. "You are being silly. Next you'll be looking under the beds."

Connie went into the living room. She sat in a chair and began to read. Still, she felt strange. She felt that something was wrong. She had the feeling that someone was staring at her. Someone in the darkness outside.

Connie walked over to the telephone. "I'm sure there is nothing wrong," she thought. "But I'll talk to someone for a while. That will make me feel better."

Connie picked up the phone. She called Mrs. Winston. Mrs. Winston lived on the other side of the lake. She was much older than Connie. Connie felt sorry for her. Mrs. Winston's life had been hard. She had many problems. When Connie talked to someone who needed help, her own troubles seemed to go away.

Mrs. Winston's voice was **cheerful** and bright.

"My dear Connie! How nice it is to have you back early!"

Connie felt better **immediately.** She said, "We had a wonderful trip. Tom is still away. He will be coming back later tonight."

Mrs. Winston sounded worried. She said, "I hope your house is all right. Is it, Connie? It's been terrible here. Did you hear?"

"No. Not a word since we left," Connie said. "What happened?"

Connie expected to hear that someone had been unkind to Charles. Charles was Mrs. Winston's only son. Connie didn't like Charles. He always seemed to be getting into trouble. He was caught stealing in school. He was thrown out of college. He kept getting into fights. Mrs. Winston said that he was just having a hard time growing up. But he was already twenty. Connie didn't care for Charles. But she did feel sorry for his mother.

Mrs. Winston's voice went on. She was telling Connie what had happened. Mrs. Winston's words hit Connie hard.

There had been several robberies in the town. The Hamiltons' house had been broken into while they were away. The same thing had happened to the Blairs and the Craigs. And Saddler's shop had been robbed one night. The robbers took his watches and his cameras.

Connie's throat was dry. She said, "I'm sorry to hear about this. Tom won't be back until about midnight."

"But, my dear," Mrs. Winston said. "You mustn't stay there alone. What if they think that the house is empty? I'll find Charles. I'll have him come for you right away. You can spend the evening here. Then Charles can take you back when Tom gets home. At least there will be two of you in the house then."

Connie said, "Oh, no! That would be silly. I'm quite all right."

Connie hung up the phone. She moved to the stairs and looked at the darkness above. She decided that she had no reason to be afraid. She would not give in to foolish fear.

She took a suitcase. Then she climbed up the stairs. She went into the bedroom and turned on the light. She put down the suitcase. Then she looked around.

Something caught her eye. There was a newspaper on the chair. Connie picked up the newspaper. She stared at it. It had yesterday's date! Someone had been in the room! Someone had sat in that chair! Someone had been there reading that paper!

For a moment Connie could not move. Her body had turned to stone.

Connie looked around the room again. There was no one there. Connie looked at the bed. What was under the bed? Could someone be hiding under the bed?

Connie backed away from the bed. She sat down in the chair. Then she got up. She looked under the bed. There was no one there.

But *something* was there!

It was a large, heavy bag. Connie dragged out the bag. She emptied it onto the floor. There were cameras and watches. There were necklaces, bracelets, and rings. The cameras and watches must have come from Mr. Saddler's shop. The other things must have come from the houses that were robbed.

Connie stood there shocked. Her house had been used as a hiding place! The robbers had put those things there. But if they found out that she was back—

The lights in the house were on! The lights could be seen across the lake! They would know she was home!

Connie turned off the bedroom light. She turned off the light in the hall. She went downstairs. She made sure the front door was locked. She turned off the light in the living room. She went into the kitchen and found some matches. She might need them in the dark. Then she turned off the kitchen light. As it went off, she noticed the back door. It was not fully closed!

She stood there in darkness. She must get to the phone! She must call the police!

Connie made her way slowly across the room. There was a sound at the back door! Then she heard footsteps.

She was at the telephone now. But she could not speak. Her voice would tell where she was.

Then she saw a soft **glow.** The man at the back door was holding a flashlight. He knew that she was in the house! He knew that she was hiding somewhere!

He went into the living room. She saw the glow of the light. He came back into the kitchen. He came toward the door. He came through the door. He was only three feet away! But she slipped quietly behind him. He did not think to turn around.

As he moved, she saw his face. She recognized him! She knew who he was!

He went into the dining room. He went into the kitchen and stood there listening. Then he went up the stairs.

Connie could not get out the front door. She would have to unlock it. But he had not closed the back door. She made her way toward it.

Then she was outside. There were stars above. She stepped onto the

grass and began to run.

She saw a motorcycle near the garage. It was his. She looked at the motorcycle. Then she had an idea. She found the gasoline cap and took it off. Then, with all her **strength,** she pushed the motorcycle and knocked it over. Gasoline ran out. It flowed onto the grass.

Connie reached into her pocket. She took out a match. She lit it. Then she dropped the match and quickly ran.

Connie hid in the shadows and watched. The flames from the gasoline leaped up. The fire would be seen across the lake. They would know that the fire was at Connie's house. Help would come soon. There would be many people and fire engines.

The flames grew higher and higher. Then a man came running out of the house. He ran toward the fire. He tried to put it out. But that was not possible.

Now cars were moving toward the house. Connie saw their headlights. She heard fire engines. Connie looked back at the fire. The man was gone.

But it did not matter. They would find out that he owned the motorcycle. They would find the stolen goods in the house. And Connie had seen his face. She knew who he was!

Connie was safe. Still, she felt sad. She felt sad for the Hamiltons and for the Blairs and for the Craigs. Their homes had been robbed. She felt sad for Mr. Saddler too. But Connie felt sorry for Mrs. Winston most of all. For Connie had seen the robber's face. And Connie knew he was Charles.

# LOOKING FOR FACTS IN THE STORY.

How well can you find facts in a story? Put an x in the box next to the right answer.

1. Connie's house was
   - ❑ a. on top of a hill.
   - ❑ b. very noisy.
   - ❑ c. alone on one side of a lake.

2. Some homes in the neighborhood had been
   - ❑ a. sold.
   - ❑ b. robbed.
   - ❑ c. burned in a fire.

3. How old was Charles?
   - ❑ a. sixteen
   - ❑ b. eighteen
   - ❑ c. twenty

4. What did Connie find under the bed?
   - ❑ a. a body
   - ❑ b. a bag
   - ❑ c. nothing

| ☐ | x 5 = | ☐ |
|---|---|---|
| **NUMBER CORRECT** | | **YOUR SCORE** |

# EXAMINING VOCABULARY WORDS.

Here are four vocabulary questions. Put an x in the box next to the right answer. The vocabulary words are printed in **boldface** in the story. You may look back at the words before you answer the questions.

1. Her voice was cheerful and bright. The word *cheerful* means
   - ❑ a. soft.
   - ❑ b. sad.
   - ❑ c. happy.

2. She heard Mrs. Winston's voice and immediately felt better. The word *immediately* means
   - ❑ a. at once.
   - ❑ b. later.
   - ❑ c. never.

3. Connie saw the flashlight glow. The word *glow* means
   - ❑ a. handle.
   - ❑ b. light.
   - ❑ c. colors.

4. Connie used her strength to push over the motorcycle. The word *strength* means
   - ❑ a. mind.
   - ❑ b. power.
   - ❑ c. fingers.

| ☐ | x 5 = | ☐ |
|---|---|---|
| **NUMBER CORRECT** | | **YOUR SCORE** |

## A ADDING WORDS TO A PARAGRAPH.
Complete the paragraph below. Fill in each blank with one of the words in the box. Each word appears in the story. There are five words and four blanks, so one word in the box will not be used.

The largest _____
                        1
in North America is Lake Superior.

Part of this lake is in the United

States, while the _____
                              2
part is in Canada. All together, Lake

Superior covers _____
                            3
31,750 square miles. At its deepest

point, Lake Superior is 1,330

_____ deep.
        4

| about | other | worried |
| lake | feet | |

## R READING BETWEEN THE LINES.
These questions will help you think critically. You will have to think about what happened in the story, and then figure out the answers. Put an *x* in the box next to the right answer.

1. Connie started the fire to
   ❑ a. get Charles out of the house.
   ❑ b. bring help quickly.
   ❑ c. frighten Mrs. Winston.

2. Which sentence is true?
   ❑ a. Mrs. Winston didn't care about her son.
   ❑ b. Connie didn't enjoy her trip.
   ❑ c. Connie didn't want to give in to "foolish fear."

3. The stolen things were probably still in the house because
   ❑ a. Connie came home a day early.
   ❑ b. Charles forgot about them.
   ❑ c. Charles didn't want them.

4. The story shows that Connie
   ❑ a. was very weak.
   ❑ b. was very unfriendly.
   ❑ c. could take care of herself.

| | x 5 = | |
| NUMBER CORRECT | | YOUR SCORE |

| | x 5 = | |
| NUMBER CORRECT | | YOUR SCORE |

26

**N**OTING STORY ELEMENTS. Some story elements are **plot, character, setting,** and **mood.** Put an *x* in the box next to the right answer.

1. What happened last in the *plot*?
   - ❑ a. Connie set the gasoline on fire.
   - ❑ b. Connie called Mrs. Winston.
   - ❑ c. The robber began to search for Connie.

2. Who is the *main character* in the story?
   - ❑ a. Connie
   - ❑ b. Mrs. Winston
   - ❑ c. Charles

3. Which sentence best *characterizes* Charles?
   - ❑ a. He was friendly and well liked.
   - ❑ b. He kept getting into trouble.
   - ❑ c. He always did well in school.

4. What is the *setting* of the story?
   - ❑ a. a garage
   - ❑ b. a beautiful garden
   - ❑ c. a house near a lake

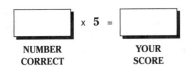

NUMBER CORRECT   × 5 =   YOUR SCORE

**THINKING MORE ABOUT THE STORY.** Your teacher might want you to write your answers.

◆ After Connie heard about the robberies, do you think she should have left the house? Give reasons for your answer.
◆ How do you think Charles decided which places to rob?
◆ Why did Connie feel so sorry for Mrs. Winston? Did you feel the same way? Why?

Use the boxes below to total your scores for the exercises. Then write your score on pages 138 and 139.

|     |     |
| --- | --- |
| [ ] | **L** OOKING FOR FACTS IN THE STORY |
| + | |
| [ ] | **E** XAMINING VOCABULARY WORDS |
| + | |
| [ ] | **A** DDING WORDS TO A PARAGRAPH |
| + | |
| [ ] | **R** EADING BETWEEN THE LINES |
| + | |
| [ ] | **N** OTING STORY ELEMENTS |
| ▼ | |
| [ ] | **SCORE TOTAL:** Story 2 |

# 3
# *Mean Rocky*

by George Shea

W hat? Are you crazy? You're wasting your time! He hates kids!"

"I don't care," said Eddie. "I'm going to get it."

My friend Eddie usually gets what he wants. Eddie collects autographs. He gets famous baseball players to sign their names for him. They sign them in his autograph book. They sign them on scorecards and baseballs. Sometimes they just sign them on pieces of paper. Eddie saves all of them. He has a big **collection.**

But he didn't have Mean Rocky Dean's autograph. Maybe nobody did. Rocky *never* gave autographs.

"I'm going to get Rocky's," he said. "I'll get it this Saturday."

"You haven't got a chance," I said. I really didn't think he had a chance. Mean Rocky Dean was the meanest guy in baseball. He really was. He was *always* getting into trouble.

But Mean Rocky was a **terrific** ballplayer. Last year, Rocky hit 42 home runs. He also hit 16 other players. He started 17 fights, 6 of them turned into riots, and he was thrown out of 22 games.

Rocky hated umpires. He hated pitchers. He hated everybody he played against. (Some people said he even hated everybody he played *with.*) He hated newspaper reporters. He hated TV reporters too. Once, he hit one over the head with a microphone.

And he hated kids, especially kids who asked for autographs. Once a kid **shoved** an autograph book through the window of Rocky's car. Rocky tore up the book.

"The guy's a monster," I said. "He'll eat you alive!"

"I don't care," said Eddie. "I'm going to get his autograph."

"How are you going to get it?" I asked.

"Don't worry. I'll get it," he said. "You can help me."

"You're crazy," I said.

I didn't know how crazy Eddie was until that Saturday.

Eddie and I went to the game together. On the way, Eddie pointed out Mean Rocky's car to me. It was in a parking lot next to the ballpark. "That's where we'll wait for him after the game," Eddie told me.

"I just hope Rocky has a good game," I said. "If he has a good game, then maybe he'll feel good. Then maybe he'll be nice to us."

"Yeah," said Eddie. "Maybe."

Maybe nothing. Rocky had a terrible game. He struck out three times and he dropped a fly ball. In the ninth inning, he came to bat with the bases loaded. He hit into a double play and his team lost the game. He was awful. I think it must have been the worst game of his life.

"Forget about it," I said, as we left the ballpark. "Now he'll give us **grief** for sure. It isn't worth it—for one stupid autograph."

"It is for Rocky's," said Eddie. "That's one important autograph. *Nobody* ever gets Rocky's autograph. But *I* will."

We headed for Rocky's car. "Here," said Eddie. He handed me a key.

"What do I do with this?" I asked.

"Just put it in your pocket," he said.

We got to Rocky's car. Eddie took out a long steel chain. It had a lock at the end of it. He ran the chain around his body a few times. There was still a lot of chain left over.

"What are you doing?" I asked.

"I'm chaining myself to Rocky's car," he said.

Now I really wanted to run. Eddie really was nuts. Rocky came along. Sure enough, he was really friendly.

"Hey, punk, get away from the car!" he said to Eddie.

"Not until I get an autograph," said Eddie.

"I'll give you an autograph—right in the mouth!" said Rocky. He took a step toward Eddie. "Now get away from my car!"

"I can't!" said Eddie. "See, I'm *chained* to it. My friend's got the key. Just sign an autograph and my friend will unlock the lock. See, just sign."

Rocky didn't sign the book. Well, not right away, anyway.

What he did do was wrap the loose end of the chain around Eddie's neck. He pulled on it—just a little. He wasn't really hurting Eddie. But Eddie was scared.

"Now unlock the chain, punk!" Rocky shouted.

I couldn't take it anymore. The whole thing was nuts. Eddie was nuts. Rocky was nuts. I *had* to stop it.

"Rocky!" I yelled. "Take it easy. I've got the key. I'll unlock it right now!" I held up the key and started to walk toward the car. Rocky loosened his grip on the chain.

Just then, a couple of newspaper reporters came by. They had cameras. One of them said, "Hey! It's Rocky Dean!"

"Who's the kid, Rocky?" one of the reporters asked. He held up his camera to take a picture.

Now the last thing Rocky wanted was his picture in the paper, especially a picture of him choking a kid. Suddenly Rocky let go of the chain. He smiled and put his arm around Eddie.

"The kid's a

good friend of mine," he said.

Rocky shook Eddie's hand. The reporters started taking pictures. Eddie was smiling. He and Rocky were smiling like crazy. They really looked like good friends.

"What's that chain for?" one of the reporters said.

"Just a little joke," said Rocky.

He and Eddie laughed. I couldn't believe what happened next. Eddie handed Rocky his autograph book. Rocky *signed* it. I couldn't believe it. I unlocked the chain.

Rocky closed the book and handed it back to Eddie. We were all still grinning away like crazy. Rocky got into his car. "Good luck, everybody!" he called out. Then he drove away.

The reporters stayed around.

"Hey, is Mean Rocky *really* a friend of yours?" one of them asked.

"Oh, sure," said Eddie. "See?" He held up the autograph book. "He just signed my autograph book!"

"Hey, that's right!" said a reporter. "That's big news! Rocky has never given an autograph before! Let's get a picture of that autograph!"

"Sure!" said Eddie proudly. He held up the book for the cameras. He opened it to where Rocky had signed.

There it was—in Rocky's own handwriting:

*

## LOOKING FOR FACTS IN THE STORY.
How well can you find facts in a story? Put an *x* in the box next to the right answer.

1. Eddie wanted to get Mean Rocky Dean's
   - ❑ a. bat.
   - ❑ b. glove.
   - ❑ c. autograph.

2. Eddie chained himself to
   - ❑ a. a fence.
   - ❑ b. a seat in the park.
   - ❑ c. Rocky's car.

3. Rocky said that Eddie was his
   - ❑ a. friend.
   - ❑ b. enemy.
   - ❑ c. brother.

4. Rocky let the reporters
   - ❑ a. ride in his car.
   - ❑ b. take pictures of him with Eddie.
   - ❑ c. shake his hand.

## EXAMINING VOCABULARY WORDS.
Here are four vocabulary questions. Put an *x* in the box next to the right answer. The vocabulary words are printed in **boldface** in the story. You may look back at the words before you answer the questions.

1. Eddie had a big collection of players' names. A *collection* is
   - ❑ a. a letter from someone.
   - ❑ b. a player's cap.
   - ❑ c. a group of things.

2. Rocky hit 42 home runs. He was terrific. The word *terrific* means
   - ❑ a. very bad.
   - ❑ b. very good.
   - ❑ c. very young.

3. A kid shoved an autograph book through the window of Rocky's car. The word *shoved* means
   - ❑ a. signed.
   - ❑ b. pushed.
   - ❑ c. closed.

4. Rocky had a poor game. That was a reason for grief. When you feel *grief,* you feel
   - ❑ a. sad.
   - ❑ b. lucky.
   - ❑ c. happy.

❑ x **5** = ❑

**NUMBER CORRECT**    **YOUR SCORE**

❑ x **5** = ❑

**NUMBER CORRECT**    **YOUR SCORE**

**A**DDING WORDS TO A PARAGRAPH. Complete the paragraph below. Fill in each blank with one of the words in the box. Each word appears in the story. There are five words and four blanks, so one word in the box will not be used.

Every _____
1
thousands of people travel to

Cooperstown, New York. They go

there to visit a _____
2
museum, the National Baseball

Hall of Fame. In the Hall are

_____ of the greatest
3
players who ever lived. You can

also see the gloves, the caps,

and the bats of some of the

_____ .
4

| baseball | pictures | year |
|---|---|---|
| | window | players |

| | x **5** = | |
|---|---|---|
| NUMBER CORRECT | | YOUR SCORE |

**R**EADING BETWEEN THE LINES. These questions will help you think critically. You will have to think about what happened in the story, and then figure out the answers. Put an *x* in the box next to the right answer.

1. Which sentence is true?
   - ❑ a. Mean Rocky always played well.
   - ❑ b. Mean Rocky never signed autographs.
   - ❑ c. Mean Rocky liked everyone.

2. Eddie thought that Rocky would give him an autograph if Eddie
   - ❑ a. begged for it.
   - ❑ b. paid him for it.
   - ❑ c. agreed to unlock the chain.

3. When Eddie saw the name that Rocky wrote, Eddie probably felt
   - ❑ a. pleased.
   - ❑ b. excited.
   - ❑ c. disappointed.

4. It is fair to say that Mean Rocky
   - ❑ a. tricked Eddie.
   - ❑ b. helped Eddie.
   - ❑ c. liked Eddie.

| | x **5** = | |
|---|---|---|
| NUMBER CORRECT | | YOUR SCORE |

**N**OTING STORY ELEMENTS.
Some story elements are **plot, character, setting,** and **mood.** Put an *x* in the box next to the right answer.

1. What happened last in the *plot*?
   - ❏ a. Mean Rocky smiled and put his arm around Eddie.
   - ❏ b. Eddie and his friend went to a baseball game.
   - ❏ c. Mean Rocky struck out.

2. Which word *characterizes* Rocky?
   - ❏ a. helpful
   - ❏ b. friendly
   - ❏ c. unfriendly

3. What is the *setting* of the story?
   - ❏ a. a newspaper office
   - ❏ b. the parking lot by a baseball field
   - ❏ c. Eddie's house

4. What is the *theme* of the story?
   - ❏ a. Some baseball players are very nice.
   - ❏ b. Two boys go to a baseball game.
   - ❏ c. A boy's plan to get an autograph fails.

[   ] x **5** = [   ]

NUMBER CORRECT          YOUR SCORE

**THINKING MORE ABOUT THE STORY.**
Your teacher might want you to write your answers.

◆ Were you sorry that Eddie didn't get Mean Rocky Dean's autograph? Why?

◆ Should Rocky have signed his real name in Eddie's autograph book? Explain.

◆ Suppose that you were one of the reporters at the scene. Would you have written a story about what happened? Give reasons for your answer.

Use the boxes below to total your scores for the exercises. Then write your score on pages 138 and 139.

[   ]  **L** OOKING FOR FACTS IN THE STORY
+
[   ]  **E** XAMINING VOCABULARY WORDS
+
[   ]  **A** DDING WORDS TO A PARAGRAPH
+
[   ]  **R** EADING BETWEEN THE LINES
+
[   ]  **N** OTING STORY ELEMENTS
▼
[   ]  SCORE TOTAL: Story 3

# 4

# The Three Brothers and the Treasure

by José Maria Eça de Queiroz

Years ago, in Portugal, there lived three brothers. Their names were Rui, Pablo, and Miguel. They were the laziest, most worthless young men in their village.

The brothers lived in an old house made of clay. It was on the side of a mountain. One winter day there was a terrible storm. The storm **destroyed** the roof of the house. It broke all the windows. The brothers had no money to fix the house. So they stayed in their freezing kitchen all winter. They sat and stared at the fireplace. No fire had burned there for a very long time.

When night came, the brothers ate a meal of black bread. Then they made their way through the snow to the stable. They slept there in the straw. During the night they heard wolves howling outside. The brothers were very poor. And their **poverty**

made them fiercer than the wolves.

Finally spring came. One morning the brothers got on their mules. They rode into the woods. They were hoping to catch some rabbits for food. Or maybe they could find some fruit. It would taste good with the black bread.

Suddenly the brothers came upon a cave. The cave was carved into a large rock. It was hard to see the cave because the rock was hidden by thick bushes.

The brothers pulled out their knives. They cut through the bushes. Then they entered the cave. Inside the cave they saw an old iron chest. The chest had three locks. And in each lock was a key.

The brothers quickly opened the locks. They threw open the chest. They saw that the chest was filled with pieces of gold!

The brothers were delighted when they saw this treasure. They laughed. They shouted. They danced wildly about.

Finally, they faced one another. They did not speak. But their looks seemed to say, "What shall we do with this gold?"

Rui was the oldest of the three. He said, "Brothers, we must divide this gold equally."

Pablo and Miguel thought that was fair. Rui said, "But this chest is very heavy. We cannot move it now. We are tired. We have not eaten all day."

Rui turned to Pablo. He was the youngest of the three. Rui said, "Take one piece of gold. Put it in your pocket. Ride into town. Buy three large leather bags to carry the gold. Buy three loaves of bread and three pieces of meat. Buy three bottles of wine. Remember, too, to buy some oats for the mules. When you return, we will eat. Then we will take home the gold. It is wise to leave after dark when no one can see us."

Miguel nodded. "That is a good idea," he said. "Pablo. Take one piece of gold and go."

Pablo stood looking down at the shining gold. He did not move. Finally he said, "The chest has three parts. Each part locks with a different key. I will lock my part. And I will take my key with me."

"Then I will lock my part of the chest too," said Miguel. "And I will keep the key."

"And I will do the same thing," said Rui.

So each brother locked his part of the chest. And each put the key safely in his pocket.

Pablo was satisfied. He said good-bye. He got on his mule. He made his way back through the woods. As he rode away, Miguel and Rui could hear him singing.

There was a grassy field across from the place where the cave was hidden. Miguel and Rui sat down on the grass. From there they kept watch over the treasure.

After a while Rui said, "Life is strange. Pablo did not want to go out today. Suppose he had stayed at home. You and I would have discovered this gold. There would have been no need to share it with him."

"True," Miguel said sadly. "How true."

Rui said, "Suppose Pablo had come along this way alone. Suppose *he* had found this gold. I am sure that he would not have shared it with us."

"That is so, brother," said Miguel. "Pablo is

greedy. Last year Pablo tricked a merchant out of many silver coins. I asked Pablo to lend me a coin to buy a new knife. He would not lend it to me."

"You see!" Rui said excitedly. "You see!"

"And how quickly Pablo wasted his silver coins!" Miguel said. "He will quickly waste this gold too."

Both men were silent for a while. Then Rui said, "You know, Pablo is a very sick man. His cough gets worse and worse. I do not think he will live until next winter."

"That is true," said Miguel.

"But by then," said Rui, "he will have spent his share of the gold. He will have wasted that **precious** gold that should be ours!"

Miguel thought for a moment. Then he said, "But suppose *we* had that money. We could rebuild our house. You would have fine clothes. You would have a handsome horse. And you would have the biggest room. You are the oldest brother. You should have the best."

"You are right!" exclaimed Rui.

Both men jumped to their feet. They suddenly had the same idea. Miguel asked slowly, "What do you think we should do?"

Rui did not answer at once. He took his brother by the arm. He drew him along the path in the woods. Then he said, "Look over there, Miguel. That is a good place—behind those bushes. You must do it, Miguel! One blow with your knife—and Pablo will be no more!"

"Yes," Rui went on, "You must do it, Miguel! Besides, Pablo makes fun of you behind your back. He calls you a fool. He calls you a good-for-nothing fool."

Miguel's face grew red with anger. "I will do it!" he growled.

"Come, then," said Rui.

They waited behind the bushes. It was a beautiful spring day. A stream flowed nearby. Birds sang. The bright sun warmed the sweet-smelling air. Miguel took the knife from his belt. He held it in his hand.

Rui looked up at the sun, which was beginning to set. He wondered what time it was. Crows flew over the trees. Miguel watched the birds disappear. He complained about how long Pablo was gone. "Pablo wastes time in town," Miguel said. "And we must wait here, hungry and thirsty."

At last! They heard the sound of a song. It was the same song that Pablo was singing when he left for town.

They saw Pablo riding up the path. There were some packages tied to his mule. Miguel moved quietly through the bushes. As Pablo passed by, Miguel raised his knife. He brought it down quickly. Pablo fell to the ground. The terrible deed was done!

"The key!" cried Rui.

From the pocket of the dead man, Rui took

the key. Rui led the mule away. Miguel walked to the stream to wash his knife. A moment later Rui was at Miguel's side.

"I will open the packages now," said Rui. "Let us eat something before we do anything more."

Rui took out his knife. Then as Miguel leaned over the stream to wash his face, Rui struck him with his knife.

Miguel slipped forward into the stream. As Miguel fell, Rui grabbed the dead man and pulled the key out of his pocket.

All three keys to the chest were now his. They were his alone! Rui took a deep breath. He was filled with joy. He opened a package and sat down on the ground. He ate some of the meat. He drank some wine. He gave each of the mules some oats. Then he packed the gold into the three large leather bags. He threw one bag over each mule. Then he started for home.

The journey took a long time, for the gold was heavy. But Rui was not in a hurry. Now and then he rested in the darkness.

Rui arrived home before the sun was up. Then he went down to the cellar of the house. He planned to bury the gold there.

Rui opened one of the bags of gold. He let the gold coins slip through his fingers. He heard the coins rattle on the stones of the floor. How lovely the gold was! What a pretty sound it made. And it was his—all his!

Now Rui was very hungry. He went outside. The sun was just beginning to rise. In the **dim** light he saw a small package. It was tied to Pablo's mule. Rui had not noticed it before. What could it be?

Rui opened the package. Ah, what delights were there! He saw turkey, fruit, sweet cakes, and chocolate. And there was a small bottle of wine. This must be a very fine wine! Pablo had probably planned to keep this fine food and wine all to himself. The greedy, selfish fellow!

Rui took the food and wine down to the cellar. He thought, "How good it is to eat as much as I want. I am glad that I do not have to share this food with my brothers."

Rui sat on the floor. He ate. As he ate, he made plans. He would rebuild the old house. Everything would be of the very best. He would wear the best clothes. He would meet the best people. He might marry a wealthy lady. She would be someone from a fine, old family.

When he finished eating, Rui picked up the small bottle of wine. He went up to the kitchen and returned with a glass. He poured some of the wine into the glass. The wine smelled very sweet. He had never before tasted good wine. Rui took a long drink. Then he waited for a while, the better to enjoy it.

Suddenly, flames of fire seemed to burn inside him! The flames tore him apart! He rose and hurried outside. He rushed to drink from the brook. He tried to cool his burning throat. But that did not help. The more he drank, the more terrible was the fire in his throat!

He began to run. On and on he ran. His throat was on fire! Suddenly he stopped by the edge of a stream. There was the body of his brother, Miguel!

Rui turned away from the body and ran. He ran across a

field. He tripped. He landed on his hands and knees. He crawled along the grass, moaning in pain. Just then he saw something on the path in the grass. It was the body of his brother, Pablo!

Suddenly Rui understood it all. It was all clear to him now. He thought about the delicious food. He thought about that small bottle of wine. Then Rui suddenly understood Pablo's terrible plan!

Rui got to his feet. He looked down at his brother on the grass. *"Poisoner! Murderer!"* Rui shouted at Pablo. Then Rui breathed his last breath and fell to the ground.

It was true. The bodies were soon found. The police discovered that Pablo had bought some poison in town. He said he wanted to rid the old house of rats. But he had put the poison into the bottle of wine. Then he put the bottle with the very best food. He was sure that his brothers would take the best food and wine. Then he—he alone—would live to get the three keys. He alone would live to have the treasure.

## LOOKING FOR FACTS IN THE STORY.
How well can you find facts in a story? Put an *x* in the box next to the right answer.

1. What did the brothers find in the woods?
   - ❑ a. fresh fruit
   - ❑ b. some rabbits
   - ❑ c. a cave

2. What was true of the chest?
   - ❑ a. It was new.
   - ❑ b. It had three locks.
   - ❑ c. It was made of wood.

3. Rui told Pablo to buy
   - ❑ a. fine clothes.
   - ❑ b. a handsome horse.
   - ❑ c. bread, meat, and wine.

4. Where did Rui plan to bury the gold?
   - ❑ a. in the cellar
   - ❑ b. in the woods
   - ❑ c. in a grassy field

## EXAMINING VOCABULARY WORDS.
Here are four vocabulary questions. Put an *x* in the box next to the right answer. The vocabulary words are printed in **boldface** in the story. You may look back at the words before you answer the questions.

1. A storm destroyed the roof. The word *destroyed* means
   - ❑ a. missed.
   - ❑ b. broke.
   - ❑ c. climbed.

2. The brothers had no money. Their poverty made them fierce. The word *poverty* means
   - ❑ a. being poor.
   - ❑ b. being rich.
   - ❑ c. being ill.

3. Pablo thought that the precious gold should be his. Something that is *precious* is
   - ❑ a. shiny.
   - ❑ b. old and small.
   - ❑ c. worth a lot.

4. In the dim light, he noticed a package. The word *dim* means
   - ❑ a. very warm.
   - ❑ b. very beautiful.
   - ❑ c. not bright.

[ ] x **5** = [ ]

NUMBER CORRECT     YOUR SCORE

[ ] x **5** = [ ]

NUMBER CORRECT     YOUR SCORE

# A
**ADDING WORDS TO A PARAGRAPH.**
Complete the paragraph below. Fill in each blank with one of the words in the box. Each word appears in the story. There are five words and four blanks, so one word in the box will not be used.

For as long as anyone can

_____ , people

<sub>1</sub>

have searched for buried gold.

These _____

<sub>2</sub>

hunters use maps and old

stories to decide where to dig.

Very few people have ever

_____ any gold.

<sub>3</sub>

Still, this does not stop others

from searching for

_____ treasure.

<sub>4</sub>

> treasure    remember    buried
>
> journey    discovered

# R
**READING BETWEEN THE LINES.**
These questions will help you think critically. You will have to think about what happened in the story, and then figure out the answers. Put an *x* in the box next to the right answer.

1. How did Rui die?
   - ❑ a. He drowned in a stream.
   - ❑ b. He was killed with a knife.
   - ❑ c. He drank wine that had poison in it.

2. We may infer (figure out) that Pablo planned to
   - ❑ a. kill his brothers.
   - ❑ b. build a new house.
   - ❑ c. give his gold to the poor.

3. Rui and Miguel thought that Pablo would
   - ❑ a. spend his gold wisely.
   - ❑ b. spend his gold quickly.
   - ❑ c. spend his gold slowly.

4. The story had an unhappy ending because the brothers
   - ❑ a. lived in a house.
   - ❑ b. did not share their treasure.
   - ❑ c. never spoke to each other.

| x 5 = | |
|---|---|

**NUMBER CORRECT**     **YOUR SCORE**

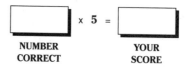

**NUMBER CORRECT**     **YOUR SCORE**

# N OTING STORY ELEMENTS.

Some story elements are **plot, character, setting,** and **mood.** Put an *x* in the box next to the right answer.

1. What happened first in the *plot*?
   - ❑ a. Pablo returned from town.
   - ❑ b. The brothers discovered a chest filled with gold.
   - ❑ c. Rui felt a burning in his throat.

2. Which words *characterize* the three brothers?
   - ❑ a. lazy, selfish, fierce
   - ❑ b. happy, honest, hardworking
   - ❑ c. friendly, helpful, liked

3. Where is the story *set*?
   - ❑ a. in Portugal, years ago
   - ❑ b. in a town in France
   - ❑ c. in the United States

4. What is the *theme* of the story?
   - ❑ a. You are lucky to find a treasure.
   - ❑ b. Rich people are not always happy.
   - ❑ c. Greed leads to the death of three brothers.

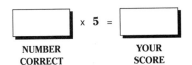

NUMBER CORRECT  × 5 =  YOUR SCORE

---

**THINKING MORE ABOUT THE STORY.** Your teacher might want you to write your answers.

◆ Do you think the three brothers "got what they deserved"? Explain.

◆ Rui said that Pablo had a very bad cough. Was Pablo so sick that he would have died before the winter? Why?

◆ Suppose that Miguel had not killed Pablo. How do you think the story might have ended? What lesson or lessons does the story teach?

Use the boxes below to total your scores for the exercises. Then write your score on pages 138 and 139.

L **OOKING FOR FACTS IN THE STORY**

+

E **XAMINING VOCABULARY WORDS**

+

A **DDING WORDS TO A PARAGRAPH**

+

R **EADING BETWEEN THE LINES**

+

N **OTING STORY ELEMENTS**

▼

**SCORE TOTAL:** Story 4

# 5

# *His Best Time*

by Elizabeth Van Steenwyk

L enny put on his running shoes. Then he started his stretching exercises. Up, down, up, down. "What good does any of this do?" he wondered, as his leg muscles gradually loosened. "I'm not getting anywhere on the track team. I might as well quit."

He continued to loosen up. He hoped Mom wouldn't hear him through his closed bedroom door. If she knew he was going to run tonight, she would be angry. No, not angry—scared. She was certain that there were dangers waiting for him out there. Dangers! Ha! What a laugh!

Now he slipped out of his room, down the stairs, and through the hall. So far, so good. He opened the front door.

"Lenny? Where are you going?" Mom called from the living room.

"Just out," he said.

Her voice came closer. "You're going out? At this hour?" She appeared at the end of the hall. "Lenny!" She saw that he was wearing his running clothes. "You're not going to run now. Not this late."

"Why does she do this to me?" he wondered. She was always treating him as if he were a kid who didn't know the score.

"Mom," he said. "I run at night because it's cooler then. You know that. Half the team runs at night. So most of the time I'm running with the other guys. Nothing is going to happen." He started out the door.

"Lenny, be careful," Mom said. Then she called after him, "Don't run for too long."

Lenny headed for the parkway down the middle of Main Street. It was a good place to run. The team used it during the day for regular workouts. And at night some of the guys on the team ran there. As Lenny ran, he felt the soft grass under his feet. His legs moved in a steady pumping motion. He breathed easily.

Then he asked himself the question he always asked when he ran at night. "If training is this easy, why can't I ever win a race?" As he turned off the street onto the parkway, he thought, "Maybe I really ought to quit."

When he went out for track, he just wanted to make one of the school's teams. There weren't that many kids on the track team. So he figured he had the best chance of making that team. After all, what was there to running? He had two legs and a good set of lungs. And he knew how to run. There was nothing to it. Right?

Wrong. He hadn't counted on Coach and on all the miles he had to put in. He didn't know there would be such stiff competition to keep a place on the team. He didn't realize that the other runners would be that good. For months he had been trying to **improve.** But nothing seemed to work. He was probably going to lose his place on the team. Maybe he should quit now. What was the point anyway?

As he ran, he noticed how quiet it was. Where was everybody? Was he that late tonight? Well, he had waited until after the 11 o'clock news began. Maybe it *was* a little later than usual. Well, he would just do a few easy miles and then go home. There was no sense in burning himself out if he was going to quit.

Coach often talked to him about his attitude. "You can make a breakthrough anytime you want to try," the coach had told him one day. "I think you have the ability. But you don't practice hard enough. You've got to try harder."

"But I *am* trying, Coach," Lenny remembered saying.

"No, you're not," Coach had said. "You're not trying at all. You *think* that you're trying. But you're not trying hard enough."

"What does he think *this* is?" Lenny thought, as he decided to pick up his speed a little. "Yeah. What does he think this is—a ride on the merry-go-round?"

Lenny was opposite the big bank now. He looked across the street at the clock above the door. This was the place where he began his timed mile. He and the other guys always started from this spot. They ran down Main Street to the bank on the other side of town. The distance was exactly one mile. It was a good way to check your time when you ran.

Lenny glanced over at the clock to see the time. Then he said to himself, "Okay. Ready. Set. *Go!*"

He ran at a steady, easy speed. "I have to pace myself," he said. "That way I'll have plenty of strength left at the end of the race if I need it."

Boy, he really felt good tonight. He was running by the post office already. A quarter of a mile was gone and he hardly felt a thing. Maybe he'd dare to pick up his speed just a little. He used his arms now, pumping them up and down. He felt a little sweat on his face. His heart began to beat a little faster. It was so quiet, the only sound that he heard was his own breathing.

He ran past the large windows of the grocery store. As he did, he thought he saw another reflection there. "But how could that be?" he thought. "How could there be another reflection if no one else is running but me?"

He suddenly had the feeling that he wasn't alone. Was that the

51

reflection of someone who was running behind him? Or was he just jumpy because Mom's talk about danger was making him nervous? "Relax," he told himself. "Just take it easy and relax."

He continued to run, feeling a little funny. Then, without breaking his rhythm, he turned slightly. In the shadows, he saw a large dog. It was running about half a block behind him. Lenny felt a sense of relief. It was nothing but a dog. Dogs often ran with the team just for the fun of it. Maybe this was one of those dogs.

Lenny turned to look at the dog. But he didn't recognize it. As the dog got closer, Lenny could see just how large the dog was. As a matter of fact, the dog was huge. What kind was he?

Now there was another dog, the same kind of dog, running next to the first one. What kind were they? They looked sort of wild. They looked like wolves he had seen in movies. Suddenly Lenny didn't like their looks at all. A shivery feeling ran up his back. He began to run faster.

He was halfway through his mile now and running quite fast. Why didn't someone else show up, even someone he didn't know? He didn't like the idea of those two dogs running swiftly and silently behind him. Why didn't they bark? Why were they so eager to catch up to him?

Lenny looked again. They were closing in on him now. He saw saliva dripping from their tongues. Their teeth flashed in the streetlight's **glare.** Their eyes never left his body. Now they were close enough for Lenny to hear them growling.

Suddenly Lenny understood. They were coming after *him!* They weren't running just for the pleasure of running. Those dogs **intended** to tear him apart! He had heard of that happening. He had heard of dogs that once were pets, dogs that suddenly turned mean and vicious—that turned into killers!

Lenny ran as hard as he could. Sweat streamed from him as he pumped his legs. He kept running as fast as he could. Still, he felt as though he were stuck in mud. No matter how hard he pushed himself, the dogs kept gaining. What would it feel like to be torn apart? What would it feel like to be ripped to shreds by those strong, sharp teeth?

What could he do? Nobody was around. Nothing was open. There were no places that he could run into for safety. It was up to him now, if he was going to escape.

"Think!" he screamed to himself. "Think!"

He heard the dogs' **savage** growling clearly now. He even thought he could feel their hot breath on his legs. He tried to think of something. All the while, he continued to run as fast as he could.

Think! What do you do with dogs like these? What do you do with dogs that run out of control like this?

He didn't know much about them. Mom never let him have a dog. She said that if he got a dog, he'd have to train the dog and make it obey.

Make it obey! Lenny thought of something! His neighbors had a dog. They had taken it to a school where he had watched them train it.

Now the dogs were right behind him. He only had a second or two in which to act. "Now!" he told himself. "Do it now!"

Lenny turned and jumped high into the air. He thrust both his arms in front of him as he came down. He screamed with every ounce of strength he had in his body. *"Stay!"* he screamed at the dogs. *"Stay! Staaaaaaaay!"*

The moment seemed frozen in time. But the dogs sat down. They stayed—as they had been taught to do a long time ago. It worked! Lenny almost collapsed with relief. It worked!

With his arms still stretched in front of him, he backed away slowly from the dogs. He made sure never to take his eyes off the dogs. He backed away from them until he was about 50 feet away.

"Hey, you there. What are you doing?" someone called. He hadn't heard the police car drive up along side of him. Lenny glanced up. He saw that he was across the street from the bank. He had run a mile. When he noticed the time on the clock, he could hardly believe his eyes. The clock said 11:19.

"Officer, would you mind driving me home?" Lenny asked. On the way back, he explained what had happened.

Lenny got out of the police car in front of his house. He went inside. He walked down the hall toward the lights in the living room. At first he hoped that Mom would be asleep. Then he changed his mind. He was glad Mom was waiting up for him now.

"Is that you already, Lenny?" she asked, without looking up from the television set. "You're back early."

"Yes," Lenny said quietly. He paused for a moment, enjoying the words he was about to say. "I did my best time ever in the mile tonight."

"That's nice," she said. "I'm glad."

"So am I," he answered. "For a lot of reasons!"

## L OOKING FOR FACTS IN THE STORY.
How well can you find facts in a story? Put an *x* in the box next to the right answer.

1. Lenny's mom was worried because Lenny was
   - ❑ a. doing poorly in school.
   - ❑ b. planning to leave the team.
   - ❑ c. going out to run at night.

2. Coach said that Lenny
   - ❑ a. was trying too hard.
   - ❑ b. wasn't trying hard enough.
   - ❑ c. was going to lose his place on the team.

3. How far was it from one bank to the other?
   - ❑ a. half a mile
   - ❑ b. one mile
   - ❑ c. two miles

4. Lenny stopped the dogs from attacking him by
   - ❑ a. running into a store.
   - ❑ b. climbing over a fence.
   - ❑ c. jumping up and shouting, "Stay!"

## E XAMINING VOCABULARY WORDS.
Here are four vocabulary questions. Put an *x* in the box next to the right answer. The vocabulary words are printed in **boldface** in the story. You may look back at the words before you answer the questions.

1. Lenny had been practicing for months. He wanted to improve. The word *improve* means
   - ❑ a. quit.
   - ❑ b. start.
   - ❑ c. get better.

2. In the streetlight's glare, Lenny saw the dogs. A *glare* is
   - ❑ a. a bright light.
   - ❑ b. a shadow.
   - ❑ c. a mirror.

3. He suddenly realized that the dogs intended to tear him apart. The word *intended* means
   - ❑ a. forgot.
   - ❑ b. planned.
   - ❑ c. hated.

4. Lenny heard a savage growl. The word *savage* means
   - ❑ a. friendly.
   - ❑ b. wild.
   - ❑ c. silent.

| | x **5** = | |
|---|---|---|
| **NUMBER CORRECT** | | **YOUR SCORE** |

| | x **5** = | |
|---|---|---|
| **NUMBER CORRECT** | | **YOUR SCORE** |

Complete the paragraph below. Fill in each blank with one of the words in the box. Each word appears in the story. There are five words and four blanks, so one word in the box will not be used.

Roger Bannister was the first

person to run a _____
1
in less than 4 minutes. On May 6,

1954, Bannister _____
2
a mile in 3 minutes 59.4 seconds.

About a month later, another

_____ , John Landy,
3
broke Bannister's record. Since

then, many runners have run a mile

in _____ 4 minutes.
4

| under | team | ran |
| mile | runner | |

R EADING BETWEEN THE LINES. These questions will help you think critically. You will have to think about what happened in the story, and then figure out the answers. Put an *x* in the box next to the right answer.

1. Lenny ran so hard that night because he wanted to
   - ❏ a. please Coach.
   - ❏ b. stay ahead of the dogs.
   - ❏ c. get home early.

2. The story shows that Lenny
   - ❏ a. was a very slow runner.
   - ❏ b. always ran as hard as he could in practice.
   - ❏ c. didn't always run as hard as he could in practice.

3. We may infer (figure out) that the dogs listened to Lenny because
   - ❏ a. they were afraid of him.
   - ❏ b. they liked him.
   - ❏ c. they remembered what they had been taught.

4. Probably, Lenny will now
   - ❏ a. become a better runner.
   - ❏ b. leave the team.
   - ❏ c. run only once in a while.

```
┌──────┐        ┌──────┐
│      │  x 5 = │      │
└──────┘        └──────┘
NUMBER           YOUR
CORRECT          SCORE
```

```
┌──────┐        ┌──────┐
│      │  x 5 = │      │
└──────┘        └──────┘
NUMBER           YOUR
CORRECT          SCORE
```

# N OTING STORY ELEMENTS.

Some story elements are **plot, character, setting,** and **mood.** Put an *x* in the box next to the right answer.

1. What happened last in the *plot?*
   - ❑ a. Lenny backed away slowly from the dogs.
   - ❑ b. Mom asked Lenny where he was going.
   - ❑ c. Lenny looked at the clock and began to run.

2. Who is the *main character* in the story?
   - ❑ a. Lenny
   - ❑ b. Mom
   - ❑ c. Coach

3. Where is the story *set?*
   - ❑ a. a school
   - ❑ b. a bank
   - ❑ c. a parkway on Main Street

4. Which word tells the *mood* of the story?
   - ❑ a. funny
   - ❑ b. serious
   - ❑ c. sad

**THINKING MORE ABOUT THE STORY.** Your teacher might want you to write your answers.

- ◆ Coach said that Lenny could "make a breakthrough at any time." What did Coach mean? Did Lenny make "a breakthrough"? Explain your answer.
- ◆ Lenny told his mom that he was glad he did his best time that night. Then Lenny added, "For a lot of reasons!" What were some of the reasons?
- ◆ What did Lenny learn about himself? About Coach?

Use the boxes below to total your scores for the exercises. Then write your score on pages 138 and 139.

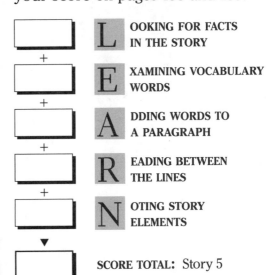

L OOKING FOR FACTS IN THE STORY

+

E XAMINING VOCABULARY WORDS

+

A DDING WORDS TO A PARAGRAPH

+

R EADING BETWEEN THE LINES

+

N OTING STORY ELEMENTS

▼

**SCORE TOTAL:** Story 5

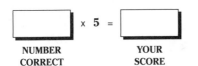

x **5** =

**NUMBER CORRECT**          **YOUR SCORE**

## 6

# *The Attic Door*

by Judith Bauer Stamper

Rosalyn pushed open the old iron gate in front of the house. The gate banged shut behind her as she walked up to the front door. Rosalyn pressed the doorbell. She waited. She could hear someone walking inside the house. A few seconds later, the front door opened.

"Rosalyn. It *is* you, isn't it?" Then she was hugged warmly by her aunt.

"Hello, Aunt Harriet," said Rosalyn.

"Come inside, dear. Come out of this heat. The house always stays cool inside."

Rosalyn followed her aunt into a large, dark hallway. It was as cool as an underground cave.

"Here you are. You're finally visiting me after so many years. How was the train ride?"

Aunt Harriet didn't wait for an answer. She **chattered** on. "I've been asking your father to let you come here for years. I know that your father didn't like my husband, Arthur. But dear Arthur has been dead for four years now."

Aunt Harriet paused and

sighed. "Yes. It has been four long years since Arthur died."

Rosalyn stared down at her feet. She didn't know what to say. Her mother had warned her that Aunt Harriet might be a little strange. Her mother was right.

"This is an **enormous** house, Aunt Harriet," Rosalyn finally said. "It has so many rooms."

"I'll show you around once you've had time to unpack. But now you'll want to see your bedroom."

"See your bedroom. See your bedroom," a high voice repeated.

"Who was that?" Rosalyn asked uneasily.

Aunt Harriet laughed. She walked to a corner of the room. Then she pulled a bright green cloth off a stand. There sat a parrot in a cage.

"That was Polly. Wasn't that you, Polly?" Aunt Harriet said. Then she made bird noises to the parrot.

Rosalyn didn't go over to the cage. She didn't like parrots. "Aunt Harriet," said Rosalyn, "I think I'll go to my room now. If you could show me where it is."

"Of course, Rosalyn." Aunt Harriet turned to the bird. "I'll be back in a few minutes, Polly."

Aunt Harriet led the way up the stairs. She walked to the room at the end of the hall.

"This is your room, Rosalyn. I hope you like it. It used to be my room when I was first married."

Rosalyn peeked inside. The whole room was done in purple. The blanket on the bed was purple. The wallpaper had purple flowers. Even the furniture had been painted purple.

"Oh, Aunt Harriet." That was all Rosalyn could think of to say.

"Put your things away, dear. Then come down. We'll have tea together."

A little later, Rosalyn came down the stairs to join her aunt for tea. Aunt Harriet was waiting in a room off the hall. Tea and cake were on the table.

"Have some of this delicious cake, Rosalyn. It's so nice to have company. Polly and I usually have to eat alone. Don't we, Polly?"

"Eat alone. Eat alone," squawked the bird from the other room.

Rosalyn ate some of the cake and sipped her tea. She looked slowly around the room. Everything looked so old-fashioned. The walls were covered with pictures of Aunt Harriet's family. One picture, in particular, caught Rosalyn's eye. It was a picture of a boy.

"Is that your son, Herman?" asked Rosalyn.

Aunt Harriet coughed. Then a terrible choking sound came from Aunt Harriet's throat.

"I'm sorry, Aunt Harriet," Rosalyn said quickly. "I shouldn't have asked you that. That was **rude** of me."

Rosalyn knew that Herman had disappeared many years ago. He had disappeared

suddenly. He had never been found. Rosalyn knew that Aunt Harriet must feel terrible about that.

Rosalyn tried to make up for upsetting her aunt. Rosalyn said, "I wish I had known Herman better. I'm sorry that I only met him a few times."

By now Aunt Harriet felt a little better. "Yes, dear," she said. "But let's not talk about the past. If you're finished eating, I'll show you the rest of the house."

Rosalyn followed her aunt out of the room. They were in the hallway again.

Aunt Harriet said, "First I want to show you your Uncle Arthur's laboratory. That was where he did his work. Arthur was a great scientist, you know. He was far ahead of his time.

"Yes," Aunt Harriet continued. "Arthur was way ahead of his time. The people at the university were very jealous of him. That was the reason he had to leave the school. But he carried on his experiments at home."

Rosalyn had known that Uncle Arthur was a scientist. But her parents never talked about his work. Rosalyn knew there had been a problem. She knew that he was forced to leave his job.

"What did Uncle Arthur study?" asked Rosalyn.

"Mutations," answered Aunt Harriet. "Ways of changing human beings."

They had walked into a large room. In the corners were piles of old books. The room was filled with large glass jars. There were chemicals in the jars. Rosalyn saw test tubes everywhere.

Aunt Harriet looked around the room. She said, "This laboratory must be kept just the way that Arthur left it. Arthur was a great man, Rosalyn. Someday everyone will know that."

"Yes, Aunt Harriet," Rosalyn said. She followed her aunt out of the laboratory. They walked into the hall again.

Aunt Harriet said, "You can look around the rest of the house by yourself. But I must make one thing very clear." Aunt Harriet's voice grew hard. "Never go up to the attic. Do you understand that, Rosalyn?"

"Do you understand that, Rosalyn?" said the parrot in the next room.

Aunt Harriet said, "I mean that, Rosalyn. Never open the door that leads up to the attic. If you do, you will be sorry!"

"You will be sorry!" Polly said.

"I understand, Aunt Harriet," said Rosalyn.

Rosalyn spent the next days wandering around the house. She looked through some old books she found. The old books reminded her of Uncle Arthur. He studied mutations, she remembered—ways of changing human beings. She sat in the garden with her aunt. Aunt Harriet sometimes talked about Uncle Arthur. But she never mentioned Herman.

The time passed pleasantly enough for Rosalyn. But after a while, she began to get **bored.** There was no one to talk to but Aunt Harriet.

The fourth day she was there, Aunt Harriet said, "Today I'm going to visit a friend. Would you like to come along?"

Rosalyn thought

about it. She said to herself, "That won't be too interesting." She told her aunt, "I think I'll stay at home. I can sit in the garden and read."

After her aunt left, Rosalyn went up to her room. She tried to read a book she had brought from home. But she didn't like it very much. After a while, she closed the book. Rosalyn got up and went out into the hall. She couldn't think of anything to do. Her vacation was turning out to be disappointing.

Rosalyn walked down the hallway. She passed the door that led up to the attic. Rosalyn stopped in front of the door. Aunt Harriet had acted so strangely about the attic. She certainly didn't want Rosalyn to go up there.

Rosalyn asked herself, "What could be up there?" Probably just old clothes and things. Rosalyn put her hand on the doorknob. To her surprise, the doorknob turned. She quickly took her hand away. Aunt Harriet had warned her not to go up there.

Rosalyn began to walk away. But she was curious about the attic. Aunt Harriet *was* a little strange. Rosalyn thought, "There's probably no reason at all why I shouldn't go up there."

Suddenly Rosalyn made up her mind. She put her hand on the doorknob and turned it. The door stuck for a moment. Then it swung open.

There were stairs that led up to the attic. Rosalyn slowly walked up the steps. When she reached the top, Rosalyn saw something horrible. She stared at the thing—the awful thing! She let out a terrible scream. Then she hurried back down the attic stairs.

Rosalyn felt sick. She couldn't believe what she had just seen. It was some horrible, furry beast!

Rosalyn pushed open the attic door. She ran down the hall. Then she heard what she had feared. Steps were coming after her. They were the footsteps of that thing!

For a moment Rosalyn was too frightened to move. The awful creature came nearer! It reached out a fur-covered arm! Rosalyn ran.

She ran down the steps. She nearly fell. The thing was coming closer! Rosalyn ran into the living room.

Then she realized that there was no way out of the room. She ran back out. She just missed the thing's outstretched arm.

Rosalyn ran into the kitchen. The thing ran after her.

Rosalyn tried to get its face out of her mind. It was the face that bothered her most. It was a strangely *human* face. She seemed to recognize that face!

Rosalyn ran through the kitchen. If only she could get to the front door! But she didn't make it there. She stumbled and fell.

Just then the front door opened. There stood Aunt Harriet. Aunt Harriet looked down at Rosalyn. Then she looked at the furry creature.

"Rosalyn!" said Aunt Harriet. "What did I tell you about going into the attic! I told you not to go up there!"

Aunt Harriet shook a finger at Rosalyn. "You've made poor Herman nervous now."

"You've made poor Herman nervous now," the parrot said.

"Poor, poor Herman," Aunt Harriet said. "He has never been the same since Arthur's last experiment." Then Aunt Harriet gently patted her son Herman's head.

Aunt Harriet looked down at Rosalyn again. "I'm sorry, Rosalyn," she said. "But you know we can't let you go—not now that you know our secret!

I'll call your parents. I'll tell them that you never arrived. You'll have to stay here in your room."

Rosalyn looked up into Aunt Harriet's face.

"But you'll be very happy here with us," Aunt Harriet said.

"But you'll be very happy here with us," repeated the parrot.

**L**OOKING FOR FACTS IN THE STORY.
How well can you find facts in
a story? Put an *x* in the box next to
the right answer.

1. Uncle Arthur had been dead for
   - ❏ a. four years.
   - ❏ b. five years.
   - ❏ c. ten years.

2. The color of Rosalyn's room was
   - ❏ a. red.
   - ❏ b. green.
   - ❏ c. purple.

3. Rosalyn was not supposed to go
   - ❏ a. into the garden.
   - ❏ b. into the attic.
   - ❏ c. out of the house.

4. Aunt Harriet said that Uncle
   Arthur was
   - ❏ a. very foolish.
   - ❏ b. very old.
   - ❏ c. a great man.

**E**XAMINING VOCABULARY WORDS.
Here are four vocabulary questions. Put an *x* in the box next to the
right answer. The vocabulary words
are printed in **boldface** in the story.
You may look back at the words
before you answer the questions.

1. Aunt Harriet didn't wait for an
   answer. She chattered on. The
   word *chattered* means
   - ❏ a. continued to walk.
   - ❏ b. continued to talk.
   - ❏ c. continued to eat.

2. The house was enormous. It had
   many rooms. The word
   *enormous* means
   - ❏ a. very large.
   - ❏ b. very small.
   - ❏ c. new.

3. Rosalyn should not have asked
   about Herman. That was rude.
   The word *rude* means
   - ❏ a. wise.
   - ❏ b. helpful.
   - ❏ c. not polite.

4. Rosalyn was alone and bored.
   The word *bored* means
   - ❏ a. pleased.
   - ❏ b. not interested.
   - ❏ c. afraid.

| | x 5 = | |
|---|---|---|
| **NUMBER CORRECT** | | **YOUR SCORE** |

| | x 5 = | |
|---|---|---|
| **NUMBER CORRECT** | | **YOUR SCORE** |

# A ADDING WORDS TO A PARAGRAPH.
Complete the paragraph below. Fill in each blank with one of the words in the box. Each word appears in the story. There are five words and four blanks, so one word in the box will not be used.

People like to have parrots as pets because a _____
1
can be taught to talk. Some parrots can _____ words
2
and sentences. But other parrots almost _____ say
3
anything. It is hard to know if the _____ is the
4
parrot, or the person who has taught it.

| parents | never | parrot |
| reason | repeat | |

|  | x 5 = |  |
| --- | --- | --- |
| NUMBER CORRECT | | YOUR SCORE |

# R READING BETWEEN THE LINES.
These questions will help you think critically. You will have to think about what happened in the story, and then figure out the answers. Put an *x* in the box next to the right answer.

1. Which sentence is true?
   - ❑ a. Rosalyn loved her aunt.
   - ❑ b. Everyone liked Uncle Arthur.
   - ❑ c. Herman was probably changed into a beast by Uncle Arthur.

2. Aunt Harriet probably kept Herman in the attic because
   - ❑ a. he liked it there.
   - ❑ b. she didn't want anyone to see him.
   - ❑ c. he was afraid of people.

3. Rosalyn seemed to recognize the creature's face because she
   - ❑ a. had met Herman years ago.
   - ❑ b. visited Herman often.
   - ❑ c. was Herman's friend.

4. We may infer (figure out) that Aunt Harriet planned to
   - ❑ a. keep Rosalyn in the house.
   - ❑ b. send Rosalyn home.
   - ❑ c. set Herman free.

|  | x 5 = |  |
| --- | --- | --- |
| NUMBER CORRECT | | YOUR SCORE |

# NOTING STORY ELEMENTS.

Some story elements are **plot, character, setting,** and **mood.** Put an *x* in the box next to the right answer.

1. What happened last in the *plot*?
   - ❑ a. Aunt Harriet showed Rosalyn the laboratory.
   - ❑ b. The creature ran after Rosalyn.
   - ❑ c. Rosalyn had tea and cake with Aunt Harriet.

2. Which sentence best *characterizes* Herman?
   - ❑ a. He was a furry beast with a strangely human face.
   - ❑ b. He was like most boys his own age.
   - ❑ c. He was a handsome young man.

3. What is the *setting* of the story?
   - ❑ a. a garden
   - ❑ b. a farm
   - ❑ c. a house

4. The *mood* of the story is
   - ❑ a. funny.
   - ❑ b. joyful.
   - ❑ c. frightening.

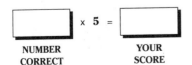

x **5** =

NUMBER
CORRECT

YOUR
SCORE

---

**THINKING MORE ABOUT THE STORY.**
Your teacher might want you to write your answers.

◆ Everyone thought that Herman disappeared many years ago. What do you think really happened?

◆ Why do you think Uncle Arthur lost his job? Give as many reasons as you can.

◆ Do you think that Rosalyn's parents will find Rosalyn? Explain your answer.

Use the boxes below to total your scores for the exercises. Then write your score on pages 138 and 139.

L OOKING FOR FACTS IN THE STORY

+

E XAMINING VOCABULARY WORDS

+

A DDING WORDS TO A PARAGRAPH

+

R EADING BETWEEN THE LINES

+

N OTING STORY ELEMENTS

▼

**SCORE TOTAL:** Story 6

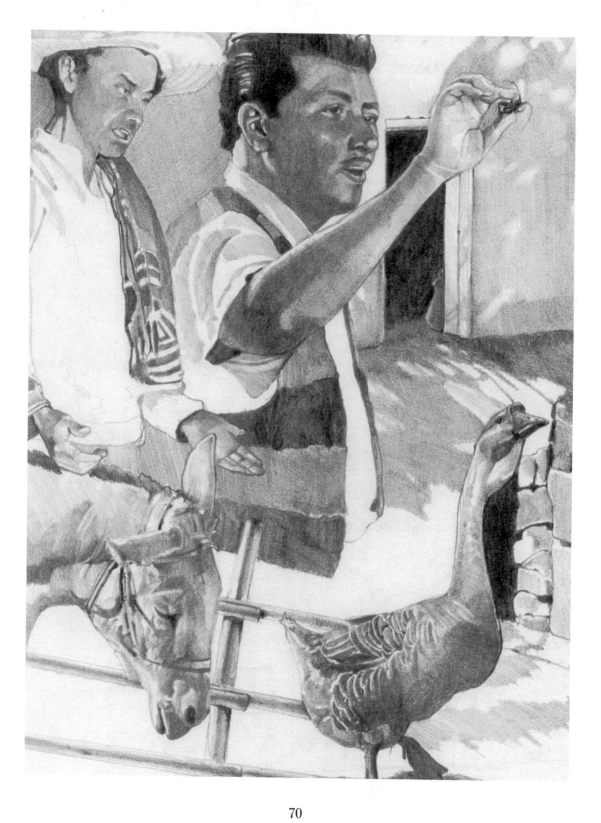

# 7

# *The Cricket*

retold by Joe Hayes

This is a story about two men who were *amigos*, which means they were friends.

One man was very rich. He had a fine ranch with many cattle. And he had a mule that was his pride and joy. It was a prize-winning mule.

His *amigo* was very poor. And he was lazy. He never worked, and he never paid his bills on time. And he was always talking and talking and talking. The people gave him a nickname. They called him *El Grillo,* which is Spanish for "The Cricket." They called him The Cricket because he was never quiet, just as a cricket won't be quiet when you're trying to fall asleep at night.

One of the foolish

things that The Cricket said was that he was *un adivino,* a seer. A seer is a person who can see into the future. So The Cricket said that he was a seer. He said that he could solve mysteries and find things that were lost. He used that idea to play a trick on his rich *amigo.*

Whenever The Cricket got far behind in his bills and owed a lot of money, he would go out to his rich *amigo's* ranch. He would catch that prize-winning mule. Then he would hide it.

The rich man would look all over his ranch for the mule. Then he would go to see The Cricket. "Can you help me?" the rich man would ask. "My mule is lost. I can't find him anywhere on the ranch. Could you use your powers as a seer to find my mule?"

The Cricket would say, "Oh, that doesn't sound too hard to do. I think I can solve this mystery. I think I can find your mule. But, you know, I need some help too. Could you pay off a few of my bills?"

The rich man would pay The Cricket's bills. Then the poor man would go back to the mountains. He would get the mule and lead it home. He played this trick on his *amigo* over and over. But his mischief almost caught up with him.

One day the rich man was in Santa Fe. He was visiting the Governor of New Mexico. The Governor was upset. He sighed, "I have lost a ring. I have had it ever since I was a child. I can't find it anywhere in the palace."

The rich man told him, "I can help you. I have an *amigo* who is a seer. He can solve mysteries. He can find things that are lost. I'll tell him to come here to find the ring."

So the next day The Cricket had to go to the Governor's palace to find the ring. Now The Cricket was in trouble. He would have to find something that *really* was lost. So he tried to get out of doing it.

The Governor said, "I understand that you are *un adivino.* I understand that you can find things that are lost."

"Oh, no, Your Honor," The Cricket said. "Sometimes I have been lucky. Now and then I have found things that were lost. But I wouldn't say I'm a seer. And I wouldn't say that I have any special powers."

When he heard that, the Governor became suspicious. He thought, "I

72

don't trust this man. He sounds like a **cheat**."

The Governor told The Cricket, "I am going to lock you in a room for three days. If you can tell me where the ring is at the end of that time, you'll get a rich reward. But if you fail, I'll know that you have been lying to the people. Then I'll see to it that you are punished. You will be very sorry that you lied."

So The Cricket was locked in a room. And of course he had no idea where the ring was. And he had no idea how he could find it.

Now the truth was that three of the Governor's servants had stolen the ring. On the evening of the first day, one of those servants was sent to The Cricket's room. The servant was sent there to serve the **prisoner** his dinner.

The servant entered. He put the food on the table. When The Cricket saw his evening meal, he thought to himself, "I have only three days to find the ring. It is already dinnertime, the end of the first day!"

So as the servant was leaving the room, The Cricket shook his head. Then he said softly, "*Ai!* Of the three, there goes the first!"

He meant the first of the three *days*. But when the servant heard him, he thought that The Cricket knew that he was one of the three thieves. He ran back to the other servants. "That man in the room!" he said. "He really is a seer! As I was leaving the room I heard him say, "'Of the three, there goes the first.' He knew that I was one of the thieves!"

"We can't be sure of that," the other two said. "Tomorrow a different one of us will take him his food. We'll see what he says then."

The next day a second servant took the evening meal to The Cricket's room. The Cricket looked at his dinner. He realized that he had only three days to save himself, and the second day was almost gone. As the servant was leaving, The Cricket sighed, "*Ai!* Of the three, there goes the second!"

The servant ran back to his friends. "There is no doubt about it! He knows! As I was leaving he said, 'Of the three, there goes the second.' He knew that I was one of the thieves too."

On the third day, the third servant brought The Cricket his food. The servant fell to his knees and **pleaded,** "Please don't tell the Governor! We know that you know about us. But if you tell the Governor, he'll send us away to prison for life!"

The Cricket realized what the man was talking about. "I won't turn you in," he told the servant, "if you do exactly as I say. Take the ring out to the barnyard. Throw the ring on the ground in front of the fattest goose there. Make sure that the goose swallows the ring."

The servant did as he was told.

Later the Governor sent for The Cricket. The Governor **demanded** to know where his ring was. The Cricket told him, "Your Honor, this is very strange. But I had a dream while I was in that room. In the dream I saw your barnyard where the geese are kept. And the ring was in the belly of the fattest goose!"

The Governor laughed. "How would my ring get there?" he said. But he ordered that the goose be cooked for dinner. And there in its stomach was the ring!

The Governor was very pleased. "This man really is a seer," he said. He thanked The Cricket and sent him home with gold.

The Cricket was glad to get away with that. He promised himself, "I'll never call myself a seer again!" But it wasn't that easy.

A few weeks later, the Mayor of Santa Fe was visiting the Governor at the palace. The Governor said, "There is a man who lives near here. This man is *un adivino*. He can solve mysteries and find things that are lost. He can tell you what is hidden in some secret place."

The Mayor laughed, "*Adivino,* indeed! There's no such thing."

The two men started to argue. And before long they made a bet. They bet a thousand dollars.

They agreed that the Mayor would hide something in a box. Then they would put the box on the roof of the palace. The Cricket would have to stand on the ground and tell what was inside the box.

When the morning of the bet came, the Mayor had a clever idea. He got a very big box and put a smaller box inside it. Then he put a smaller box inside that, and so on, until the last box he put in was very tiny.

"He'll think there's something very big in this large box," the Mayor laughed. "I'll get something very small to put in this tiny box."

He went out to the garden to look for something small. Just then a little cricket went hopping across the path. The Mayor caught it. He put it in the smallest box. He closed all the boxes and put them inside each other. Then he had a guard take the large box to the roof of the palace. Another guard went to get The Cricket.

The poor Cricket stood on the ground. He looked up at the roof of the palace. He had no idea what was in the box. But the Mayor of Santa Fe and the Governor of New Mexico were standing there next to him. And there were soldiers all around. He couldn't run.

He just stood there. An hour passed, and then another.

Finally the Mayor started to laugh. "This man doesn't know what is in the box. It is just as I said!" He turned to the Governor and told him, "Pay me the money."

Now the Governor grew angry. "Speak up!" he told The Cricket. "Tell us what's in the box! Speak up!" Finally he roared, "I warn you! Speak up! What's in the box?"

The Cricket had to say something. He began to stutter, "In the box . . . in the box . . . in the box . . . in the box . . ."

"What?" gasped the Mayor. "How does he know there's a box inside a box inside a box!"

And then, thinking about himself, The Cricket cried out, "Oh, no! They've got you this time, you poor little Cricket!"

The Mayor was amazed. "He knows it's a cricket! If I hadn't heard it with my own ears, I never would have believed it!" He took out his wallet. He gave a thousand dollars to the Governor of New Mexico.

The Governor gave five hundred of those dollars to The Cricket. The

Governor shook his hand and slapped him on the back. "Well done again!" he said. And he sent him home.

That was too close a call for The Cricket. He said, "Never again in my whole life will I tell anyone that I have special powers."

But the boys on his street often made fun of The Cricket. Earlier that day,

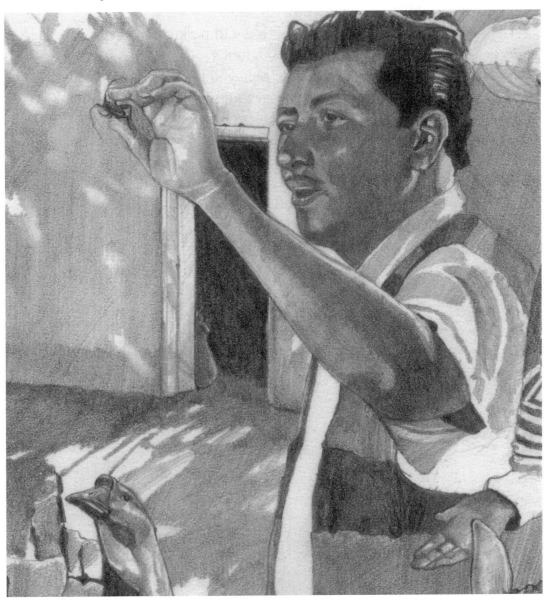

they had filled a big bag with garbage. And as The Cricket walked down the street, they ran out to meet him.

They waved the bag in front of him. *"Adivino!"* they yelled. "Use your special powers. Tell us what's inside this bag."

"Don't call me *adivino*," The Cricket said angrily. "I don't believe in that anymore. It's nothing but a bunch of garbage!"

The boys stared at him, shocked. "How did he know it was garbage? He *really* is a seer! We thought he was just a fool."

So from that day on, all the people believed that The Cricket was a seer. He kept saying, "No! I'm not a seer. I have no special powers at all!"

But no matter how hard he tried, the people wouldn't believe him. They kept coming to his house. They kept asking him to solve mysteries and to find things.

Finally, in order to have some peace, he had to move far away. He moved to a place where they hadn't heard of *adivinos,* or seers. And if The Cricket hasn't died, he must still be living there.

**L**OOKING FOR FACTS IN THE STORY. How well can you find facts in a story? Put an *x* in the box next to the right answer.

1. They called the man The Cricket because he
   - ❑ a. was very small.
   - ❑ b. ate very little.
   - ❑ c. was never quiet.

2. Why did the rich man pay The Cricket's bills?
   - ❑ a. The Cricket worked on his farm.
   - ❑ b. The Cricket found his mule.
   - ❑ c. The rich man owed him money.

3. Who took the Governor's ring?
   - ❑ a. the Mayor
   - ❑ b. the rich man
   - ❑ c. the Governor's servants

4. What did the Governor give The Cricket?
   - ❑ a. a gold ring
   - ❑ b. five hundred dollars
   - ❑ c. one thousand dollars

**E**XAMINING VOCABULARY WORDS. Here are four vocabulary questions. Put an *x* in the box next to the right answer. The vocabulary words are printed in **boldface** in the story. You may look back at the words before you answer the questions.

1. The Governor thought he was a cheat. A *cheat*
   - ❑ a. helps people.
   - ❑ b. likes people.
   - ❑ c. tricks people.

2. The Cricket was a prisoner in a room. A *prisoner* is someone who
   - ❑ a. is locked up.
   - ❑ b. has many friends.
   - ❑ c. likes to stay indoors.

3. He pleaded, "Don't tell about us!" The word *pleaded* means
   - ❑ a. hoped.
   - ❑ b. wondered.
   - ❑ c. begged.

4. The Governor demanded that The Cricket tell him where the ring was. The word *demanded* means
   - ❑ a. tried.
   - ❑ b. ordered.
   - ❑ c. wished.

| | x 5 = | |
|---|---|---|
| **NUMBER CORRECT** | | **YOUR SCORE** |

| | x 5 = | |
|---|---|---|
| **NUMBER CORRECT** | | **YOUR SCORE** |

# A DDING WORDS TO A PARAGRAPH.

Complete the paragraph below. Fill in each blank with one of the words in the box. Each word appears in the story. There are five words and four blanks, so one word in the box will not be used.

At one time or another, you have probably _____
1
the sound of a cricket. Do you

_____ how the
2
cricket makes this sound? The

_____ rubs the
3
edges of its wings rapidly together.

As it does this, it makes the

_____ which we
4
sometimes call the cricket's song.

| different | heard | cricket |
| sound | know | |

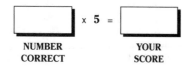

NUMBER          YOUR
CORRECT         SCORE

# R EADING BETWEEN THE LINES.

These questions will help you think critically. You will have to think about what happened in the story, and then figure out the answers. Put an *x* in the box next to the right answer.

1. The Cricket knew where the mule was because he
   ❏ a. had special powers.
   ❏ b. knew a lot about mules.
   ❏ c. hid the mule himself.

2. The Cricket discovered who took the ring because of
   ❏ a. a dream.
   ❏ b. what the servant said.
   ❏ c. something he read.

3. When The Cricket cried out, "Oh, you poor little cricket," he was talking about
   ❏ a. the cricket in the box.
   ❏ b. a cricket in his garden.
   ❏ c. himself.

4. Why did The Cricket move far away?
   ❏ a. He liked to travel.
   ❏ b. People kept bothering him.
   ❏ c. His neighbors scared him.

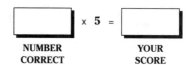

NUMBER          YOUR
CORRECT         SCORE

# N OTING STORY ELEMENTS.

Some story elements are **plot, character, setting,** and **mood.** Put an *x* in the box next to the right answer.

1. What happened last in the *plot*?
   - ❑ a. The Mayor put a cricket into a box.
   - ❑ b. They found the ring in a goose.
   - ❑ c. Some boys waved a bag in front of The Cricket.

2. The *main character* in the story is
   - ❑ a. The Cricket.
   - ❑ b. the Mayor.
   - ❑ c. the Governor.

3. Which sentence best *characterizes* The Cricket?
   - ❑ a. He liked to work hard.
   - ❑ b. He paid his bills on time.
   - ❑ c. He was foolish, clever, and lucky.

4. The *mood* of the story is
   - ❑ a. sad.
   - ❑ b. funny.
   - ❑ c. serious.

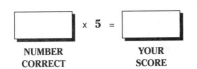

NUMBER CORRECT   × 5 =   YOUR SCORE

**THINKING MORE ABOUT THE STORY.** Your teacher might want you to write your answers.

- ◆ How did The Cricket find out who took the ring? Should he have told the Governor the truth? Explain.
- ◆ Suppose The Cricket had not discovered who took the ring. What do you think would have happened to him?
- ◆ Why did the people believe that The Cricket was *un adivino*? Why couldn't The Cricket change their minds?

Use the boxes below to total your scores for the exercises. Then write your score on pages 138 and 139.

| | |
|---|---|
| | **L** OOKING FOR FACTS IN THE STORY |
| + | |
| | **E** XAMINING VOCABULARY WORDS |
| + | |
| | **A** DDING WORDS TO A PARAGRAPH |
| + | |
| | **R** EADING BETWEEN THE LINES |
| + | |
| | **N** OTING STORY ELEMENTS |
| ▼ | |
| | **SCORE TOTAL:** Story 7 |

# 8

## *The Ghost of Wan Li Road*

by Kara Dalkey

One hot summer day, long ago in the village of Nanyang, three young men sat in the shade. They were discussing their fortune.

"I have very little money," said one. "I have not eaten in two days. My stomach is growling as loud as a dragon. I fear it will soon eat me from the inside out."

"That sounds painful, indeed," said the second. "What will you do?"

"I think," said the first, "that I will go to the forest. I will chop some wood to sell."

The third young man was named Sung Ting-Po. He was known to be very clever. He said, "That won't help you. It's summer. No one will buy wood for warmth. And the wood is very dry. It will turn to splinters as soon as your ax strikes it."

The first young man shrugged. He looked down at the dust between his feet.

"I am also very poor," said the second young man. "I have not bought new shoes in a year. Look. My toes and heels have worn through these."

"They look useless, indeed," said the first. "What will you do?"

"I will go to the lake and catch ducks for their feathers. I will then sell the feathers to the pillow maker."

But Sung Ting-Po said, "The lake is dry, my friend. And no ducks swim there now. You can't get feathers from empty mud."

The second young man sighed and stared at his hands.

The first said, "You are clever, Sung Ting-Po. What will you do to earn money? You are as poor as we are."

Sung Ting-Po skipped a stone along the dusty ground. "I think I will try my luck at the market in Wan. Perhaps I can find a merchant who needs a helper."

The other two stared at each other a moment. Then they looked at Sung Ting-Po. "Wan is very far away," said the first. "How will you get there?"

"I'll walk," said Sung Ting-Po. "I will leave this evening, when it is cool. I should reach Wan at daybreak. That is when the market opens."

"No, no!" said the other two. "You don't want to do that."

"Why not?" said Sung Ting-Po.

"That road," said the first, with fear in his voice, "is the Wan Li Road. It is guarded by a horrible ghost!"

Sung Ting-Po started to laugh.

"It's true!" said the second. "I have seen this ghost with my own eyes."

"Me too!" said the first.

"What did you do when you saw this ghost?" asked Sung Ting-Po.

"Need you ask?" said the second. "I ran home as fast as my legs could take me. I didn't want to be caught by that ghost."

"And you?" Sung Ting-Po asked the first.

"I got down on my knees. I begged the ghost not to hurt me. The ghost said he would spare my life this once. But I was never to travel the Wan Li Road again after dark or he would surely kill me."

"I see," said Sung Ting-Po with a grin. "Well, my friends, I am more afraid of starving than I am of a ghost. I don't care how horrible he looks. Your tales will not keep me from walking the Wan Li Road tonight." With that, Sung Ting-Po stood up. He dusted himself off and turned to go on his way.

"You should listen to us!" said the first.

"If you walk on that road, the only fortune you will gain is death," said the second. "We'll see," said Sung Ting-Po.

The setting moon glowed in the west, and the wind hissed through the dry grasses. Sung Ting-Po had been walking on the Wan Li Road for hours. But it had not been tiring. All he carried with him was a piece of rope in his pocket. Along the way he had seen nothing strange. The only sounds were the hooting of the night birds and the soft *pad-pad* of Sung Ting-Po's bare feet on the dust of the road. But it was only an hour after midnight. He still had very far to go.

Then he noticed a strange mist close to the ground by the side of the road. The mist drifted into the middle of the road ahead of Sung Ting-Po. It then turned into the shape of a hideous old man. Sung Ting-Po knew that this must be the ghost. This creature stared at Sung Ting-Po with a hateful eye. It opened its mouth, preparing to speak.

But Sung Ting-Po beat him to it and spoke first. "Good morning!" he said to the ghost, smiling.

The ghost shut his mouth and frowned. Then he said, "Early morning it may be. But it is not good. Not for you, young man."

"Why is that?" said Sung Ting-Po.

"Because," said the ghost. "I am a *ghost!*"

"Well, that's really amazing!" said Sung Ting-Po. "I'm a ghost too."

"You are?" said the ghost. "You look rather solid and not like a mist."

"Uh . . . that's because . . . because . . . I'm a *new* ghost," said Sung Ting-Po. "I just died tonight. In fact, I ate some bad mushrooms for dinner, and they poisoned me. I am now on my way to the market in Wan. I want to find the merchant who sold the bad mushrooms to my mother."

"Well now, well now," said the ghost. "That sounds like the right thing to do. Yes, indeed. I would like to help you. Do you mind if I come along?"

"Not at all," said Sung Ting-Po.

They walked in silence together for a while. The ghost floated above the road. But Sung Ting-Po's feet kicked up little clouds of dust as he walked.

"Say there," said the ghost. "If you *are* a ghost, why do you still walk along on the ground? Why don't you float *above* it like me?"

"Ah," said Sung Ting-Po, "I am so new at being a ghost that I still walk with my feet upon the earth. I guess I'll get over it in time. After all, you did."

"Ah, hum, well, yes. Although I don't remember having to touch the ground with my feet after I died."

"Ah, you are a very fine ghost! There is much I could learn from you," said Sung Ting-Po.

"Indeed," said the ghost. "Indeed, there is! You know, Wan is farther than I remembered. The sun will be rising before long. We want to get there before the sun comes up. Ghosts should not be caught in the sunlight. Why don't we take turns carrying each other?"

"A good idea," said Sung Ting-Po.

First Sung Ting-Po carried the ghost. This was no **burden** for him, for the ghost was very light and airy. But then came the ghost's turn to carry Sung Ting-Po.

"Ooof!" said the ghost as Sung Ting-Po climbed onto his back. "You are very heavy. Are you sure you're a ghost?"

Sung Ting-Po said, "I guess I'll get lighter as I get older. I'm still very new at being a ghost."

"Ah, hum, well, even as a new ghost I was never as heavy as you," said the ghost.

They continued in this way for some time. Then they came to a river. The ghost crossed first. He floated easily over the water like a flower petal on a summer breeze. But Sung Ting-Po splashed his way across. He made great waves in the water. He got **soaked** up to his waist.

Sung Ting-Po dripped onto the far bank of the river. The ghost said, "What a mess you are! What a noise you made! Are you *sure* you're a ghost?"

Sung Ting-Po threw up his hands. "Don't blame me! I'm still new at this. I don't know how to behave as a ghost yet. I don't know anything about ghosts. Why, I don't even know if there is anything ghosts ought to be afraid of. Does anything bother us ghosts?"

"Ah, hum, well—you need not worry. There is almost nothing we ghosts have to fear."

"*Almost* nothing?" said Sung Ting-Po. "Oh, wise one. If there is something I must **avoid,** please tell me! It would be terrible if my life as a ghost were cut short because of something I didn't know. Please, help me with your great knowledge."

"Well," said the ghost, "there is one thing. It is human breath. We ghosts don't like to be breathed on by humans. If humans breathe on us, we can't float in the air anymore. We must walk on the ground."

"Thank you," said Sung Ting-Po, bowing deeply. "I will keep that in mind."

And so they continued down the Wan Li Road. Finally, they saw the town of Wan ahead of them. But the sun was beginning to rise in the east.

"Dear me. That's too bad," said the ghost. He shook his head. "We were too slow. We cannot make it into town before daylight. We ghosts are not **permitted** to wander around in daylight, you know. We'll have to come back tonight. We'll find your merchant then. Now we must return to where we have to go. Come along." The ghost began to disappear.

"Wait!" said Sung Ting-Po. "I don't know how to get to wherever it is we have to go. Please let me hang on to your sleeve so that you can show me the way."

"Oh, very well," said the ghost. He held out his right sleeve so that Sung Ting-Po could hold on to it.

The young man did. And Sung Ting-Po twisted the ghost's arm and held the ghost tightly. The ghost could not escape.

"I have you now!" said Sung Ting-Po.

"Let me go!" cried the ghost. He tried to get out of Sung Ting-Po's grasp. But Sung Ting-Po did not loosen his grip one bit.

The ghost changed himself into a slippery frog. But still Sung Ting-Po held him. He changed into a tiger. But Sing Ting-Po did not let the tiger's teeth or claws touch him. The ghost became a bear. But still Sung Ting-Po was stronger. At last, the ghost turned into a big, black sheep. Then Sung Ting-Po breathed on him and turned him around toward the light of the sun.

"Thank you for your lesson, most excellent ghost," said Sung Ting-Po. "Now you must stay in this shape. And you must walk on the ground, just as you said."

"Baaaahh," said the ghost.

And Sung Ting-Po took the rope from his pocket. He tied the rope around the sheep's neck. Cheerfully, he led the sheep down the road into the town of Wan.

His two friends were very surprised when Sung Ting-Po returned to Nanyang. He looked well fed. He was wearing a new pair of shoes.

"Where have you been?" they asked. "How did you come by this good luck?"

"I went to the market at Wan by way of the Wan Li Road."

"The Wan Li Road! Didn't you see the ghost?"

"I certainly did," said Sung Ting-Po.

"Didn't he try to hurt you?"

"Not at all. In fact, he taught me some very useful things. But you don't have to worry. He won't be bothering anyone on the Wan Li Road any longer."

The other two young men looked astonished. "You killed the ghost?"

"Killed him? Don't be silly. I waited until he turned into a sheep. Then I sold him in the market in Wan. A fine, big, black sheep can sell for a very high price." And with that, Sung Ting-Po continued down the street. Coins jingled in his pockets. The others watched and scratched their heads in wonder.

# LOOKING FOR FACTS IN THE STORY.

How well can you find facts in a story? Put an *x* in the box next to the right answer.

1. Sung Ting-Po said that he was planning to go
   - ❑ a. into the forest.
   - ❑ b. to the lake.
   - ❑ c. to the market at Wan.

2. The two men warned Sung Ting-Po not to
   - ❑ a. chop wood during the summer.
   - ❑ b. stay up after dark.
   - ❑ c. walk on the Wan Li Road.

3. Sung said that he walked with his feet on the ground because he
   - ❑ a. enjoyed walking that way.
   - ❑ b. was still a new ghost.
   - ❑ c. wanted to be different from the other ghosts.

4. What did Sung do with the big, black sheep?
   - ❑ a. He sold it.
   - ❑ b. He killed it.
   - ❑ c. He gave it to his friends.

```
┌──────┐        ┌──────┐
│      │  x 5 = │      │
└──────┘        └──────┘
NUMBER           YOUR
CORRECT          SCORE
```

# EXAMINING VOCABULARY WORDS.

Here are four vocabulary questions. Put an *x* in the box next to the right answer. The vocabulary words are printed in **boldface** in the story. You may look back at the words before you answer the questions.

1. Sung got soaked in the water. The word *soaked* means
   - ❑ a. very angry.
   - ❑ b. very funny.
   - ❑ c. very wet.

2. The ghost was no burden to carry because he was so light. The word *burden* means
   - ❑ a. a good friend.
   - ❑ b. a heavy load.
   - ❑ c. a happy time.

3. He wanted to avoid danger. The word *avoid* means
   - ❑ a. keep away from.
   - ❑ b. try to meet.
   - ❑ c. fight with.

4. Ghosts are not permitted to wander around during the day. The word *permitted* means
   - ❑ a. needed.
   - ❑ b. allowed.
   - ❑ c. worried.

```
┌──────┐        ┌──────┐
│      │  x 5 = │      │
└──────┘        └──────┘
NUMBER           YOUR
CORRECT          SCORE
```

# A DDING WORDS TO A PARAGRAPH.
Complete the paragraph below. Fill in each blank with one of the words in the box. Each word appears in the story. There are five words and four blanks, so one word in the box will not be used.

Many people love to tell

_____ stories at
<sub>1</sub>

night by a campfire. Then, all the

_____ of the
<sub>2</sub>

evening suddenly come alive. The

shadows in the darkness can

_____ scare you.
<sub>3</sub>

You feel afraid, though you know

that there really is nothing to

_____ .
<sub>4</sub>

| sounds | market | easily |
|--------|--------|--------|
| | fear | ghost |

# R EADING BETWEEN THE LINES.
These questions will help you think critically. You will have to think about what happened in the story, and then figure out the answers. Put an *x* in the box next to the right answer.

1. Sung Ting-Po was able to get the better of the ghost by
   - ❑ a. scaring it.
   - ❑ b. tricking it.
   - ❑ c. killing it.

2. Who helped Sung the most?
   - ❑ a. the two young men
   - ❑ b. a farmer from the village
   - ❑ c. the ghost himself

3. We may infer (figure out) that the ghost
   - ❑ a. will continue to guard the Wan Li Road.
   - ❑ b. will no longer guard the Wan Li Road.
   - ❑ c. will escape from the market at Wan.

4. At the end of the story, the two men were
   - ❑ a. angry.
   - ❑ b. afraid.
   - ❑ c. amazed.

[____] x **5** = [____]

NUMBER CORRECT     YOUR SCORE

[____] x **5** = [____]

NUMBER CORRECT     YOUR SCORE

# NOTING STORY ELEMENTS.

Some story elements are **plot, character, setting,** and **mood.** Put an *x* in the box next to the right answer.

1. What happened first in the *plot*?
   - ❏ a. Sung Ting-Po met the ghost.
   - ❏ b. Sung started walking along the Wan Li Road.
   - ❏ c. Sung returned to Nanyang with a new pair of shoes.

2. Which word *characterizes* Sung Ting-Po?
   - ❏ a. clever
   - ❏ b. rich
   - ❏ c. scared

3. The story is *set*
   - ❏ a. in a village and on a road.
   - ❏ b. in a large city.
   - ❏ c. at a busy market.

4. The *mood* of the story is
   - ❏ a. very serious.
   - ❏ b. very sad.
   - ❏ c. light and amusing.

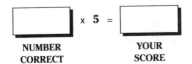

NUMBER CORRECT ☐ × 5 = ☐ YOUR SCORE

**THINKING MORE ABOUT THE STORY.**
Your teacher might want you to write your answers.

◆ Sung Ting-Po had a very quick mind. Give examples from the story that show that Sung was clever.

◆ Why do you think the ghost believed what Sung Ting-Po told him? Give as many reasons as you can.

◆ At the end of the story, Sung told his two friends what happened. Do you think they believed him? Why?

Use the boxes below to total your scores for the exercises. Then write your score on pages 138 and 139.

☐ **L** OOKING FOR FACTS IN THE STORY

+

☐ **E** XAMINING VOCABULARY WORDS

+

☐ **A** DDING WORDS TO A PARAGRAPH

+

☐ **R** EADING BETWEEN THE LINES

+

☐ **N** OTING STORY ELEMENTS

▼

☐ **SCORE TOTAL:** Story 8

# 9

# *The Family*

based on a story by Anton Chekhov

Marsha's parents were poor. They worked on a small farm near a village. Still, they managed to send Marsha to a fine school in Moscow.

After Marsha finished school, she began to look for work. One week later, she found a job. She worked for a family named Kushkin. The Kushkins were very rich. They had a cook and maids. They had many servants.

Marsha's job was to teach the children of the family. In return, she lived at the house and received some pay. Marsha did her job very well. Before long, all the children loved Marsha. She was the best teacher the family ever had.

One afternoon, Marsha went out for a walk. When she returned, a servant met her at the door. He said, "Mr. and Mrs. Kushkin are having a fight. I have never seen Mrs. Kushkin so angry. She has been yelling and screaming for almost an hour."

Marsha knew that Mrs. Kushkin had a very bad temper. Marsha thought to herself, "I will stay out of her way today."

In the hall, Marsha saw Lisa, who was one of the maids. Lisa had tears in her eyes. Then Mr. Kushkin came running down the stairs. He was a little man who had almost no hair. He was red in the face. He was shaking all over. He rushed past Marsha. He did not even see her.

Mr. Kushkin was very upset. He was saying, "Oh, this is awful. Just awful! I can't believe what she's doing. It doesn't make any sense!"

Marsha went up the stairs and stepped into her room. What she saw shocked and amazed her. Mrs. Kushkin was in her room! She was standing in front of Marsha's dresser. The drawers of the dresser were open.

Mrs. Kushkin was looking through Marsha's things! Mrs. Kushkin was *searching* through her things!

Mrs. Kushkin was surprised. "Oh," she said. "I thought you were out taking a walk. I didn't expect you to come back so soon. I seem to have knocked over some of your things. Sorry for the accident." Then she marched out of the room.

Marsha did not know what to think. What was Mrs. Kushkin doing in her room? On top of the dresser was a small wooden box. In it Marsha kept a few coins and some stamps. The box had been opened! The cover was off.

Marsha looked around. She could tell that Mrs. Kushkin had searched the whole room. Things on the table had been moved. The bookshelves, the closet, the bed—they had all been searched. But why? What was going on? What had happened?

Marsha remembered that Lisa had tears in her eyes. She thought about Mr. Kushkin rushing down the stairs. Did those things have anything to do with this search? Marsha did not know. She sank into a chair. She wondered about it all.

A few minutes later, Lisa entered the room. Marsha jumped up. "Lisa," she said. "Mrs. Kushkin has been searching my room. Do you know why?"

Lisa answered, "Mrs. Kushkin has lost one of her necklaces. It is worth two thousand rubles."

"Yes," said Marsha. "But why did she look in my room? She could not have lost it here."

"Don't you see?" said Lisa. "She thinks that one of us stole it."

"But . . . but why search here?" continued Marsha. She still did not understand.

"Mrs. Kushkin is certain that somebody stole the necklace. It's **ridiculous.** The idea! But she is searching for it everywhere."

Marsha could not believe what she heard. She was so angry she began to shake.

Lisa said, "But there's no need for you to worry, Miss. She didn't find anything here. You didn't take the necklace, so you have nothing to be afraid of."

"But . . . but this is terrible, Lisa. It's wrong! It's wrong! How dare she think I stole her necklace! What right has she to look through my things!"

"You are living among strangers," said Lisa. She sighed. "You are a teacher. You are a young lady. Still they treat you this

way. It's not like living at home with your mama and papa."

After Lisa left, Marsha was close to tears. Never before had she suffered such an insult. Imagine. They thought she might steal a necklace. They thought she might be a thief!

Suddenly, Marsha became frightened. She began to think about horrible things. They might have her arrested. They might throw her in jail. Who would be able to help her? Who would come to her side? Her parents lived far away. They could not travel to Moscow. She was alone in a big city, without family, without friends.

There was a knock on the door. "Dinner is ready," said a servant. Marsha wondered whether or not to go down. She did not want to eat with the family. But if she stayed in her room, they might think she was guilty.

Marsha went into the dining room. Dinner had already begun. Mr. Kushkin sat at one end of the table. Mrs. Kushkin sat at the other. At the sides of the table sat the children and some guests. Two servants brought out the food. Everyone knew that Mrs. Kushkin was very angry. No one said a word.

Mrs. Kushkin was the first person to speak. "What is the main course?" she asked.

"I asked them to make fish," Mr. Kushkin said. "Of course if you don't want that, the cook will make you something else. I thought that fish . . ."

Mrs. Kushkin said, "You know I don't like fish! First someone steals my necklace. Then you have them make fish!"

"There, there," said a guest. He patted her hand. "Don't be upset. Don't think about the necklace. Your health is more important than the two thousand rubles."

"I don't care about the money!" cried Mrs. Kushkin. "But I won't have a thief in my house! And I have been so kind!"

Everyone felt ashamed. They all looked down at their plates. But Marsha imagined that they were looking at her. She suddenly got up. She said, "I feel ill. I cannot finish my food. I am going upstairs."

She got up from the table and quickly went out.

Mr. Kushkin turned to his wife. "Really," he said. "There was no reason to search her room. She is not a thief."

"I do not say that she took the necklace," Mrs. Kushkin replied. "Still, you never can tell."

"But we trust her with our children," Mr. Kushkin went on. "And you know that they love her."

"I only know that my necklace is gone!" said Mrs. Kushkin. "I am going to find it! Now eat your fish, and mind your own business!"

Upstairs, Marsha was lying on the bed. She was not frightened. She was not ashamed. But she was very angry. She was thinking, "I wish that I could buy an **expensive** necklace. I would throw it in Mrs. Kushkin's face."

But that was just a dream. There was only one thing she could do. She must go away from here. She must go away quickly. She did not want to give up her job, but she could not work where people did not respect her. Marsha jumped up from the bed. She began to pack her things.

"May I come in?" asked Mr. Kushkin. He had come to the door. He spoke in a soft, **gentle** voice. "May I come in?"

"Come in," said Marsha.

Mr. Kushkin came in and stood at the door. He pointed to the suitcase. "What does this mean?" he asked.

"I am leaving. I am sorry, Mr. Kushkin. But I cannot stay in your house any longer. This search has insulted me deeply."

"I understand," said Mr. Kushkin. "But there is no need to do this. My wife searched your room. That is true. But she did not find anything. Don't let this bother you so much."

Marsha said nothing. She went on packing.

Mr. Kushkin said, "You are hurt, of course. But you know my wife. She has a terrible temper. Please don't take this so badly."

Still Marsha said nothing.

"Well, then," continued Mr. Kushkin. "I apologize to you. I am very sorry. I apologize."

Marsha didn't answer.

"That isn't enough for you? Then I apologize for my wife. I apologize for us both."

Marsha said, "I know that you are not to blame. It is not your fault. There is no need for you to worry about this."

"Of course," he said. "But, still . . . don't go away. Please stay."

Marsha shook her head and continued to pack.

Mr. Kushkin walked slowly to the window. He stared into the street. Then he said, "It is all my fault. If you leave, I'll never forgive myself. I beg you to stay!"

Marsha did not answer.

"I took my wife's necklace!" Mr. Kushkin said suddenly. "I took the necklace! Are you satisfied now?" He paused. Then he said, "Please. Don't say a word to anyone."

Marsha was **stunned.** She stared at Mr. Kushkin.

He was silent for a moment. Then he said, "She controls the money. She gives me very little. And I have bills to pay."

Just then, they heard Mrs. Kushkin's voice calling from below.

"Nicholas! Nicholas! I need your help. Come here at once! There is one more place that I want to search."

Mr. Kushkin went downstairs. Half an hour later, Marsha was on her way.

# L OOKING FOR FACTS IN THE STORY.

How well can you find facts in a story? Put an *x* in the box next to the right answer.

1. Marsha worked for the Kushkins as a
   - ❏ a. cook.
   - ❏ b. maid.
   - ❏ c. teacher.

2. The lost necklace was worth
   - ❏ a. two thousand rubles.
   - ❏ b. three thousand rubles.
   - ❏ c. five thousand rubles.

3. Mrs. Kushkin said that she hated
   - ❏ a. meat.
   - ❏ b. fish.
   - ❏ c. vegetables.

4. Who took the necklace?
   - ❏ a. Lisa
   - ❏ b. Marsha
   - ❏ c. Mr. Kushkin

# E XAMINING VOCABULARY WORDS.

Here are four vocabulary questions. Put an *x* in the box next to the right answer. The vocabulary words are printed in **boldface** in the story. You may look back at the words before you answer the questions.

1. It was ridiculous to think someone took her necklace. The word *ridiculous* means
   - ❏ a. foolish.
   - ❏ b. interesting.
   - ❏ c. good.

2. Her necklace was expensive. Something that is *expensive*
   - ❏ a. is new.
   - ❏ b. costs a lot.
   - ❏ c. costs very little.

3. He spoke to her in a soft, gentle voice. The word *gentle* means
   - ❏ a. kind.
   - ❏ b. angry.
   - ❏ c. loud.

4. When he said he took the necklace, Marsha was stunned. The word *stunned* means
   - ❏ a. very pleased.
   - ❏ b. very sorry.
   - ❏ c. very surprised.

|  | x 5 = |  |
|---|---|---|
| **NUMBER CORRECT** | | **YOUR SCORE** |

|  | x 5 = |  |
|---|---|---|
| **NUMBER CORRECT** | | **YOUR SCORE** |

**DDING WORDS TO A PARAGRAPH.**
Complete the paragraph below.
Fill in each blank with one of the
words in the box. Each word
appears in the story. There are five
words and four blanks, so one word
in the box will not be used.

Anton Chekhov is one of

Russia's _____
<br>1

known writers. He went to school

in _____ to
<br>2

become a doctor. While at school,

he wrote for a newspaper to earn

money for his _____.
<br>3

But he liked writing so much that

he decided to _____
<br>4

that his life's work.

| Moscow | worth | best |
|--------|-------|------|
| family | make | |

    [      ] x **5** = [        ]

    **NUMBER          YOUR**
    **CORRECT          SCORE**

**R**EADING BETWEEN THE LINES.
These questions will help you
think critically. You will have to
think about what happened in the
story, and then figure out the
answers. Put an *x* in the box next
to the right answer.

1. Mr. Kushkin was probably upset
   because
   ❑ a. his wife lost a necklace.
   ❑ b. a maid took the necklace.
   ❑ c. he knew that he had taken
        the necklace.

2. Which sentence is true?
   ❑ a. Marsha was rich.
   ❑ b. Mr. Kushkin asked Marsha
        to stay.
   ❑ c. Mrs. Kushkin always
        searched Marsha's room.

3. We may infer (figure out) that
   rubles must be
   ❑ a. jewels.
   ❑ b. dollars.
   ❑ c. money used in Russia.

4. Why did Marsha leave?
   ❑ a. She couldn't work for
        people who didn't trust her.
   ❑ b. She wanted more money.
   ❑ c. She had a new job.

    [      ] x **5** = [        ]

    **NUMBER          YOUR**
    **CORRECT          SCORE**

# NOTING STORY ELEMENTS.

Some story elements are **plot, character, setting,** and **mood.** Put an *x* in the box next to the right answer.

1. What happened last in the *plot*?
   - ❑ a. Marsha began to pack her things.
   - ❑ b. Marsha suddenly felt ill at dinner.
   - ❑ c. Mrs. Kushkin looked through Marsha's things.

2. Who is the *main character* in the story?
   - ❑ a. Mr. Kushkin
   - ❑ b. Mrs. Kushkin
   - ❑ c. Marsha

3. The story is *set* in
   - ❑ a. New York City.
   - ❑ b. Moscow.
   - ❑ c. Paris.

4. The *mood* of the story is
   - ❑ a. funny.
   - ❑ b. serious.
   - ❑ c. scary.

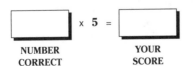

**NUMBER CORRECT**   x **5** =   **YOUR SCORE**

---

**THINKING MORE ABOUT THE STORY.**
Your teacher might want you to write your answers.

- ◆ Do you think that Mrs. Kushkin will ever discover that her husband took the necklace? Explain your answer.
- ◆ Suppose you were Marsha. Would you have stayed after Mr. Kushkin told you the truth and said he was sorry? Why?
- ◆ Do you think that Mr. and Mrs. Kushkin had a good marriage? Give some reasons and examples in your answer.

Use the boxes below to total your scores for the exercises. Then write your score on pages 138 and 139.

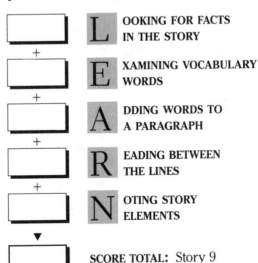

**L** OOKING FOR FACTS IN THE STORY

+

**E** XAMINING VOCABULARY WORDS

+

**A** DDING WORDS TO A PARAGRAPH

+

**R** EADING BETWEEN THE LINES

+

**N** OTING STORY ELEMENTS

▼

**SCORE TOTAL:** Story 9

# 10

# *A Helping Hand*

### by Janet Ritchie

D r. Robinson was driving along a quiet country road. Suddenly he saw something unusual up ahead. A dark blue car was parked on the side of the road.

"That's a strange place to stop," Dr. Robinson thought to himself.

Dr. Robinson slowed down. He saw that the hood of the car was up. A tall man stood next to the car. The man wore a long, heavy coat. He was looking at the motor of the car.

Dr. Robinson pushed down on the brake. He stopped in front of the blue car. The man suddenly slammed down the hood of his automobile. Then he hurried to the window of Dr. Robinson's car. Dr. Robinson had lived in the area all of his life. But he had never seen the tall man before.

"Having some car trouble?" Dr. Robinson asked.

The stranger nodded yes. He glanced up and down the road. Then he said, "There's not much traffic around here."

Dr. Robinson smiled. "You're right about that," he said. "Not much traffic at all. You could stand on this road all day. Two or three cars might come by. You're lucky I happened to be driving this way."

"I guess I am," said the man.

The stranger stared at Dr. Robinson's car. Then he said, "All right, mister. Get out of that car. And hurry!"

The man's hand was in the pocket of his coat. Dr. Robinson knew that he was holding a **weapon.**

"All right," Dr. Robinson said. "Take the car. You're welcome to it. But I can tell you this. That car is no bargain. It has gone ninety-thousand miles—most of them on these **bumpy** country roads."

"Your car will do fine," said the man. He looked closely at the doctor. "The problem is what to do with you. I'd like to let you go. I really would. But you've seen my face."

Dr. Robinson was shocked. He stared at the stranger.

"Now get out of the car, mister!"

Dr. Robinson reached across the seat. He picked up his black bag. Then he stepped out of the auto.

"What now?" asked the doctor. His heart was pounding.

But the stranger did not answer. He was looking at the black bag that the doctor was holding.

"Well," said the stranger at last. "Maybe my luck is beginning to change. It looks like I found myself a doctor."

The stranger slowly unbuttoned his coat. There was a handkerchief around his left arm. The handkerchief once had been white. It was now **stained** red.

"Take a look at my arm," said the man. "But be careful, doc. Don't do anything foolish. Remember, I've got a gun in my other hand."

Dr. Robinson lifted the handkerchief. He **examined** the man's arm. But the doctor did not speak.

The man was impatient. "Well, doc?" he asked. "What do you think?"

Dr. Robinson said slowly, "You are luckier than you know. That's a serious wound. A little deeper and you would now be dead."

Dr. Robinson put the handkerchief back in its place. Then he said, "But that bullet will have to be removed right away."

The stranger nodded. "All right, doc. Get busy."

Dr. Robinson shook his head. "No," he said. "I couldn't possibly do that here. You would start to bleed again. I don't think I would be able to stop it."

The stranger looked worried.

Dr. Robinson said, "Why don't we go to my office? Everything that I need is there. It would be easy to remove the bullet."

The stranger thought for a moment. Then he asked, "How far is your office from here?"

"About five miles, at the edge of the village. We could get there in ten minutes."

Dr. Robinson waited while the stranger made up his mind. It seemed to take forever. Finally, he motioned to the car. "All right, doc," he said. "You do the driving."

Dr. Robinson turned around. He took a deep breath. He had no plan. He did not know what he was going to do.

But he felt safer as long as the stranger needed him alive.

Dr. Robinson drove for about a mile. Then he felt the gun against his side. "Hey," the stranger said. "What's going on up there?"

A car stood in the middle of the road ahead.

Dr. Robinson forced himself to be calm. "It looks like a roadblock," he said. "That's Jim Holman's car. Jim is the sheriff around here."

Up ahead, Sheriff Holman relaxed when he saw the doctor's car.

"We'll have to stop," Dr. Robinson told the stranger. "I'll just say hello and ask what's the matter."

"All right," said the stranger. "But don't forget that I have my hand on this gun. Don't use any words that I can't understand. If you do . . ."

The stranger did not finish his thought. But Dr. Robinson knew exactly what he meant.

Dr. Robinson slowed the car to a stop. He rolled down the window.

"Hi, Jim," he said. "What seems to be the trouble?"

Jim smiled. "This is supposed to be a roadblock," he said. "But so far you're the only one to come along. Didn't you hear about the bank robbery, doc?"

Dr. Robinson shook his head. "I'm afraid not, Jim."

Jim leaned on the car. "A man tried to rob a bank up at Miller's Falls. He didn't get anything. But he and the guard fired some shots at each other. The guard is in the hospital now. The man got away in a dark blue car."

"Is that so?" said the doctor. He nodded toward the stranger. "This is a good friend of mine, Jim. I've known him for years. Say hello to Bill."

The sheriff put his hand through the open window. He said, "Jim Holman's my name. I sure am glad to meet a friend of the doc's."

The stranger kept his hand at his side. He forced himself to smile at the sheriff.

"Don't mind if Bill doesn't shake hands," the doctor said quickly. "Bill's right hand has a pretty deep cut. He got it chopping some wood. I had to go out to his place. I stitched it up there."

"I see," said the sheriff. He thought for a moment. Then he said, "You have to watch those things. Be careful about infection."

Dr. Robinson smiled. "Oh, I don't think my pal has to worry about that. We're stopping off at my office now. I'll give him some pills."

"Had a hard day?" asked Jim.

"Oh, about the same. Mostly kids with colds."

"See you around, doc," said Jim Holman. He turned to the other man. "Take care of your hand."

Dr. Robinson pulled around Jim Holman's car. Then he continued up the road. "You did fine, doc," the stranger said. He turned to look back at Jim Holman. The sheriff was inspecting the tires on his car.

Dr. Robinson kept his speed at thirty miles an hour. "Come on, doc," the stranger said. "You can go faster than this."

Dr. Robinson shook his head. He said, "The road here is pretty rough. And this car has bad springs."

In fifteen minutes they reached the edge of the village. Dr. Robinson said, "This is my driveway. I'll pull up to my garage. We can get out there."

"It's about time," the stranger said. "It took you long enough to get here."

Dr. Robinson stopped in front of the garage. "That's fine," the stranger said. "Now open your door and get out. Stand there where I can see you."

"Now!" thought Dr. Robinson. "Now is the time for Jim Holman to be here!"

The stranger pushed open the door on his side of the car. He stepped out onto the driveway.

Then he heard a loud voice behind him.

"Don't move, mister! Freeze! Drop the gun! This is the police!"

The stranger dropped the gun. Then he put up his hands.

Dr. Robinson said, "I drove as slowly as I could, Jim. I knew you'd take the other road. I figured that you would get here first."

Jim Holman took out handcuffs and slipped them over the stranger's wrists. Jim said, "I had to be careful when you were both in the car. I didn't want to try anything then. I guessed that he had a gun on you."

The stranger's voice was filled with anger. He asked, "What did the doc say? How did he tip you off?"

Jim Holman smiled as they walked up to the doctor's office. Jim said, "I didn't think that the doc had stitched up your hand. But I *knew* that he hadn't seen kids with colds all day."

The sheriff pointed to a sign in front of the doctor's office. The big letters said:

> Henry F. Robinson
> VETERINARIAN
> ANIMAL DOCTOR

## LOOKING FOR FACTS IN THE STORY.

How well can you find facts in a story? Put an *x* in the box next to the right answer.

1. The tall man was wearing
   - ❏ a. a long coat.
   - ❏ b. a light jacket.
   - ❏ c. a wool cap.

2. Dr. Robinson said that the man should go
   - ❏ a. to the hospital.
   - ❏ b. to the doctor's office.
   - ❏ c. home.

3. After Dr. Robinson went around the roadblock, how fast did he drive?
   - ❏ a. thirty miles an hour
   - ❏ b. forty miles an hour
   - ❏ c. fifty miles an hour

4. The sign said that the doctor
   - ❏ a. was on vacation.
   - ❏ b. saw people every day except Sunday.
   - ❏ c. was an animal doctor.

| | x 5 = | |
|---|---|---|
| **NUMBER CORRECT** | | **YOUR SCORE** |

## EXAMINING VOCABULARY WORDS.

Here are four vocabulary questions. Put an *x* in the box next to the right answer. The vocabulary words are printed in **boldface** in the story. You may look back at the words before you answer the questions.

1. Dr. Robinson did what the man said because the man had a weapon. A *weapon* is used for
   - ❏ a. fighting.
   - ❏ b. playing.
   - ❏ c. driving.

2. The car traveled over bumpy roads. The word *bumpy* means
   - ❏ a. smooth.
   - ❏ b. rough.
   - ❏ c. busy.

3. The handkerchief once had been white. It was now stained red. The word *stained* means
   - ❏ a. colored.
   - ❏ b. cleaned.
   - ❏ c. tied.

4. He examined the man's arm. The word *examined* means
   - ❏ a. shook.
   - ❏ b. worried about.
   - ❏ c. looked at closely.

| | x 5 = | |
|---|---|---|
| **NUMBER CORRECT** | | **YOUR SCORE** |

**DDING WORDS TO A PARAGRAPH.**
Complete the paragraph below.
Fill in each blank with one of the
words in the box. Each word
appears in the story. There are five
words and four blanks, so one word
in the box will not be used.

Have you ever

_____ a pet

  1

to a veterinarian's office? Most pets

act very frightened and

_____. Some

  2

animals try to leave as soon as they

enter the _____.

  3

Often, it is difficult for the owner

to keep the pet

_____.

  4

| worried | taken | office |
|---------|-------|--------|
| motor | calm | |

| | x **5** = | |
|---|---|---|
| **NUMBER CORRECT** | | **YOUR SCORE** |

**R**EADING BETWEEN THE LINES.
These questions will help you
think critically. You will have to
think about what happened in the
story, and then figure out the
answers. Put an *x* in the box next
to the right answer.

1. We may infer (figure out) that
   the stranger
   - ❑ a. tried to rob a bank.
   - ❑ b. cut his hand badly.
   - ❑ c. knew the roads very well.

2. Dr. Robinson was probably afraid
   that the man would
   - ❑ a. get an infection.
   - ❑ b. kill him.
   - ❑ c. sell the doctor's car.

3. Why did Dr. Robinson drive to
   his office so slowly?
   - ❑ a. His car was very old.
   - ❑ b. The road was very bad.
   - ❑ c. He wanted the sheriff to
     get there first.

4. How did Jim Holman know that
   Dr. Robinson was in trouble?
   - ❑ a. Dr. Robinson kept winking.
   - ❑ b. He gave Jim a note.
   - ❑ c. Jim knew that Dr. Robinson
     wasn't telling the truth.

| | x **5** = | |
|---|---|---|
| **NUMBER CORRECT** | | **YOUR SCORE** |

# NOTING STORY ELEMENTS.

Some story elements are **plot, character, setting,** and **mood.** Put an *x* in the box next to the right answer.

1. What happened last in the *plot*?
   - ❑ a. The stranger unbuttoned his coat.
   - ❑ b. The man dropped his gun.
   - ❑ c. Jim Holman's car was blocking the road.

2. Which sentence best *characterizes* Dr. Robinson?
   - ❑ a. He was too frightened to think clearly.
   - ❑ b. He acted cooly and calmly, although he was in danger.
   - ❑ c. He was not friendly.

3. Where is the story *set*?
   - ❑ a. on a farm
   - ❑ b. in a large city
   - ❑ c. somewhere in the country

4. What is the *theme* of the story?
   - ❑ a. A doctor's quick thinking probably saves his life.
   - ❑ b. A stranger nearly fools a sheriff.
   - ❑ c. A bank robber has trouble with his car.

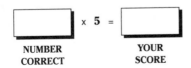

| | x **5** = | |
|---|---|---|
| NUMBER CORRECT | | YOUR SCORE |

## THINKING MORE ABOUT THE STORY.

Your teacher might want you to write your answers.

- ◆ Dr. Robinson said the bullet had to be removed right away. Was that true, or did he make that up? Explain.
- ◆ Why didn't the stranger shake hands with Jim Holman? Why did Dr. Robinson say that he had stitched up the man's hand? Give several reasons.
- ◆ Did you think that the sheriff would be waiting at Dr. Robinson's office? Why?

Use the boxes below to total your scores for the exercises. Then write your score on pages 138 and 139.

| | |
|---|---|
| | **L** OOKING FOR FACTS IN THE STORY |
| + | |
| | **E** XAMINING VOCABULARY WORDS |
| + | |
| | **A** DDING WORDS TO A PARAGRAPH |
| + | |
| | **R** EADING BETWEEN THE LINES |
| + | |
| | **N** OTING STORY ELEMENTS |
| ▼ | |
| | **SCORE TOTAL:** Story 10 |

# 11

# *The Shop*

### by H. G. Wells

I had seen the shop on the street before. I had passed by it once or twice. A sign on the door said "THE MAGIC SHOP." Another sign said "Magic Tricks Sold Here."

The window was filled with interesting things. There were glass balls. There were rabbits in hats. There were playing cards. You know—the kind that magicians use.

I had never thought about going inside. But Jimmy and I were taking a walk. He suddenly grabbed me by the arm. He pulled me up to the magic shop.

"Look, daddy," he said. "Look in the window there." He pointed a finger at a box. The words on the box said "THE DISAPPEARING EGG."

Jimmy's eyes opened wide. "If I were rich," he said, "I'd buy that trick. And that one too. And that! And *that!*"

I said, "Your birthday is only two months away. We could come back then."

But then Jimmy saw a bright blue box. A card next to it said "BUY ONE OF THESE. AMAZE YOUR FRIENDS!"

Jimmy pulled me by the arm again. He pushed open the door. We went into the store.

This was no **ordinary** store. This was a magic shop. It was not very big. It was not well lit. The door banged shut as we went inside.

We were alone. There was no one else there. Jimmy and I quickly looked around. We saw a paper tiger in a glass cage. The tiger smiled at us and shook its head.

There were magic fishbowls of every kind. There were piles of coins. There were funny mirrors everywhere. When you looked in some, you looked tall and thin. Others made you look short and fat.

While we were laughing at these, a salesperson came in. I guess he came in. I didn't *see* him come in. But there he was!

He was quite tall with a long, sharp chin. He rested his arms on the top of the counter.

"May I help you?" he asked.

"Yes," I said. "I'd like to buy a few tricks for my son."

"What kind do you want?" asked the man.

"Some that are easy and fun," I said.

"I see," said the man. Then he suddenly reached behind his head. He pulled a little glass ball out of his ear.

"Something like this?" he asked. He held out the ball.

I was surprised. I had seen that trick done before, of course. Magicians *always* do that particular trick. But I had not expected to see it here.

"That's good," I said to the man.

"Yes, isn't it?" he said.

Jimmy reached out to take the glass ball. But the ball wasn't there!

"You'll find it in your pocket," announced the man.

Jimmy reached into his pocket. And there it was!

"How much does that cost?" I asked the man.

"Oh, we do not charge for glass balls," he said. "We get them free."

He pulled another glass ball out of his neck while he spoke. Then he took one out of his other ear.

"You may have all of them free," he said. "You may have this one too." He reached up and pulled another ball out of his mouth. "Here you are!" he said.

Jimmy looked at me. "You may have them," I said.

The man turned to Jimmy. "You know," he said, "you're the right kind of boy."

"What do you mean?" I asked.

"Only the right kind of boy can come into this shop."

Just then we heard someone banging loudly on the door. Then we heard the squeaky voice of a boy. "Ny-a-a-ah!" it squealed. "I *wanna* go in there! Ny-a-a-ah! Ny-a-a-ah! I *wanna* go in there! I *WANNA* go in there!"

The boy's parents could be heard outside. "But we *can't* go in there. The door is locked."

The boy's voice trailed away. "Ny-a-a-ah!" cried the boy. "I *wanna* go in there!"

"But the door *isn't* locked," I told the man. "*We* just came in!"

"The door is locked *now,*" said the man. The door is always locked to that kind of boy!"

"How did you do that?" I asked in **astonishment.** "How could you lock the door from way over here?"

"It's magic!" said the man. "We're a real magic shop. We do real magic here. Watch this!"

The man waved his hand, and colored sparks of fire flew into the air.

I smiled at the trick. Still, I thought he was carrying the joke just a little too far.

The man turned to Jimmy and said, "You wanted the box with THE DISAPPEARING EGG."

"But . . . how did you know that?" I asked the man.

He did not answer. He just put his hand into my jacket and took out that box.

"Let's wrap the box now," said the man. He reached up into the air and some paper appeared. Then he put his hand to his mouth and began pulling out string. He kept pulling out string—it seemed never to end. Out came yards and yards of bright red string.

The man's hands danced through the air, and a moment later, the box was wrapped. There was even a beautiful ribbon on top.

Just then I felt something moving around in my hat. I took off my hat—and out flew a pigeon. It flew around the room. Then it hopped into a box next to the smiling paper tiger.

"That's strange," said the man. "Here, let me see that hat." He shook it up and down. Out popped five or six eggs and a shiny gold watch.

"It's surprising," said the man, "what people carry in their hats." He shook it some more. Out came a rabbit and a bunch of red roses.

"Are you finished?" I said. "Are you finished with my hat?"

But there was no answer. For no one was there!

I stared at Jimmy, and Jimmy stared at me.

"Daddy," said Jimmy.

"What is it?" I asked.

"I *like* this store, daddy. I like it *so* much!"

Before I could say a word, the tall man appeared. He came out of some door on the side, I suppose. He said, "May I show you our other room, sir?"

Jimmy pulled me by the arm. "*Please,* daddy," he said. And before I could answer, we were in that other room.

"Everything here is real magic," said the man. "Why, here's a magic sword. It doesn't bend. It cannot break. It's very, very sharp, but it cannot cut your fingers. Here's the best part. Whoever owns this sword will never lose a **battle**."

"Oh, daddy!" said Jimmy. "That's just what I need!"

The fellow was good. There's no question about that. He showed Jimmy magic trains. They ran by themselves without batteries or power. Then there were toy soldiers lying in a box. The soldiers came alive when you said a certain word. It's a hard word to say. I can't say it myself. But Jimmy learned it right away.

"Bravo!" cried the man when Jimmy said the word. He put the toy soldiers back into the box. "Say the word once more," said the man. Jimmy said the certain word, and the soldiers popped to life again.

"Would you like to have these soldiers?" asked the man.

"Oh, yes!" Jimmy said.

The man put the soldiers into the box and closed the top. He waved the box in the air. *Presto!* It was wrapped! And Jimmy's name and address were written on the box!

"We must go now," I said. "How much is the bill? And where is my hat?"

I looked around. Now Jimmy was gone!

"Stop this fooling!" I yelled. "Tell me, where is my boy?"

I reached out for the man. But he turned away from me and ran.

"Stop!" I called.

He ran through an open door, and I ran swiftly after him.

*Bang!*

"Excuse me, sir," said a little man. "I didn't see you there."

I was out on the street again. I had bumped into someone on the street. And there, just a few feet away, was Jimmy. He was holding a box.

I turned around to look at the magic shop. But nothing was there. There was just a little **alley.**

We did not say a word until we reached home. Jimmy spoke first. "That was *some* shop," he said. "That was *some* shop, daddy."

"Yes," I agreed.

Then we opened the box. It was filled with toy soldiers.

That happened six months ago, and now everything seems fine. Jimmy's toy soldiers seem just like any toy soldiers.

But I said to Jimmy one day, "What if your toy soldiers could come alive? What if they could march around all by themselves?"

"Oh, but mine *do,*" Jimmy said. "I just have to say a certain word before I open the box."

"Then they march around by themselves?"

"Oh, yes, daddy," Jimmy said. "I wouldn't like them as much if they couldn't do that."

Since then I sometimes drop in when Jimmy is playing. His soldiers seem just like any other toy soldiers. But it's hard to tell.

There is also the question of the bill. I want to pay for the soldiers. I guess the man at the shop will send a bill. After all, he knows Jimmy's name and address. But so far he has never sent a bill.

Since then, I have walked that street again and again. But I have never been able to find the shop. It seems to have disappeared—like magic!

**L** OOKING FOR FACTS IN THE STORY. How well can you find facts in a story? Put an *x* in the box next to the right answer.

1. What was in the window of the shop?
   - ❑ a. a paper tiger in a cage
   - ❑ b. toy soldiers in a box
   - ❑ c. a box with a "disappearing egg"

2. The tall man said that Jimmy was
   - ❑ a. a selfish child.
   - ❑ b. the right kind of boy.
   - ❑ c. very silly.

3. The toy soldiers "came alive" when you
   - ❑ a. shook them up and down.
   - ❑ b. put batteries in them.
   - ❑ c. said a certain word.

4. When did Jimmy and his father visit the magic shop?
   - ❑ a. a month ago
   - ❑ b. six months ago
   - ❑ c. a year ago

| | x 5 = | |
|---|---|---|
| **NUMBER CORRECT** | | **YOUR SCORE** |

**E** XAMINING VOCABULARY WORDS. Here are four vocabulary questions. Put an *x* in the box next to the right answer. The vocabulary words are printed in **boldface** in the story. You may look back at the words before you answer the questions.

1. It was not an ordinary shop. The word *ordinary* means
   - ❑ a. old.
   - ❑ b. usual.
   - ❑ c. closed.

2. "How did you do that?" he asked in astonishment. The word *astonishment* means
   - ❑ a. surprise.
   - ❑ b. happiness.
   - ❑ c. danger.

3. Whoever owns that sword will never lose a battle. A *battle* is
   - ❑ a. a bet.
   - ❑ b. a fight.
   - ❑ c. a soldier.

4. The magic shop was gone. All that was left was a little alley. What is an *alley*?
   - ❑ a. a tall building
   - ❑ b. a big town
   - ❑ c. a narrow street

| | x 5 = | |
|---|---|---|
| **NUMBER CORRECT** | | **YOUR SCORE** |

## A DDING WORDS TO A PARAGRAPH.

Complete the paragraph below. Fill in each blank with one of the words in the box. Each word appears in the story. There are five words and four blanks, so one word in the box will not be used.

Harry Houdini was one of the

greatest _____

                    1

who ever lived. He was able to

_____ himself from

          2

anything. He got out of ropes,

chains, and even jails into which

he had been _____.

                    3

For forty years he amazed people

everywhere with his

_____.

     4

| free | magicians | tricks |
| locked | glass | |

| NUMBER CORRECT | x 5 = | YOUR SCORE |

## R EADING BETWEEN THE LINES.

These questions will help you think critically. You will have to think about what happened in the story, and then figure out the answers. Put an *x* in the box next to the right answer.

1. Jimmy's father entered the magic shop because
   - ❏ a. he loved magic tricks.
   - ❏ b. he knew about the shop.
   - ❏ c. his son wanted to go inside.

2. We may infer (figure out) that the boy outside was
   - ❏ a. very polite.
   - ❏ b. not "the right kind" of boy.
   - ❏ c. one of Jimmy's friends.

3. What is unusual about the story?
   - ❏ a. Characters seem to appear and disappear.
   - ❏ b. All the characters are about the same age.
   - ❏ c. The story is very long.

4. Which sentence is true?
   - ❏ a. They sent Jimmy a bill.
   - ❏ b. Jimmy's father never found the shop again.
   - ❏ c. Jimmy paid for the toys.

| NUMBER CORRECT | x 5 = | YOUR SCORE |

# N OTING STORY ELEMENTS.
Some story elements are **plot, character, setting,** and **mood.** Put an *x* in the box next to the right answer.

1. What happened last in the *plot*?
   - ❏ a. Jimmy said he wanted the toy soldiers.
   - ❏ b. The man wrapped the box.
   - ❏ c. Jimmy's father bumped into a man on the street.

2. Which sentence *characterizes* the tall man?
   - ❏ a. He loved all children.
   - ❏ b. He did magic tricks well.
   - ❏ c. He made people pay high prices.

3. The story is *set*
   - ❏ a. in a small house.
   - ❏ b. in a magic shop.
   - ❏ c. in a department store.

4. What is the *theme* of the story?
   - ❏ a. Unusual things happen when a father and son go into a magic shop.
   - ❏ b. You should not buy things you do not need.
   - ❏ c. Some stores go out of business very quickly.

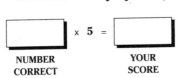

| NUMBER CORRECT | x 5 = | YOUR SCORE |

---

Use the boxes below to total your scores for the exercises. Then write your score on pages 138 and 139.

| | **L** OOKING FOR FACTS IN THE STORY |
| + | **E** XAMINING VOCABULARY WORDS |
| + | **A** DDING WORDS TO A PARAGRAPH |
| + | **R** EADING BETWEEN THE LINES |
| + | **N** OTING STORY ELEMENTS |
| ▼ | |
| | **SCORE TOTAL:** Story 11 |

## 12

# *It's So Wonderful Here*

### by Bill Pronzini

I t's so wonderful here. It's so much more wonderful than on Earth. There's golden sunshine here. And the air is warm and it tastes sweet. We have a stream on our piece of land. When you go wading, the water is so cold that it makes your toes **numb.**

There's a lot of shade too. And there are fruit trees and thick green grass. There are hundreds of different kinds of flowers. Some of the flowers are as big as I am. They have huge yellow leaves that you can use to make kites.

Kite flying is fun. And it's fun to chase the orange and green butterflies. It's fun to listen to them sing as they fly across the meadow. At night, it's fun to lie on the ground and look up at our three moons in the sky. It's fun to watch them as they bounce around.

Oh, it's so wonderful here. There's so much you can do here. You can pick berries along the banks of Big Winding River. You can go exploring in Big Woods. It stretches for miles and miles behind all the pieces of land in Section A where I live.

I like Big Woods best of all. I know all the paths, and I can go in very deep. I can go where it's dark, where the tree branches are so thick that you can't see the sky. It smells green and fresh in there. And you don't have to worry about animals or anything. You see, there's nothing in Big Woods except little pink kittens. They're friendlier than the kitten I once had back on Earth. It's fun to watch them when they hide in the leaves.

Selena and I went into Big Woods this morning. We went to pick gingery snaps. Selena lives with her parents on the piece of land next to ours. She's eleven and a half, and I'm just three months younger than she is. She has more **chores** to do because her parents make her do jobs around the house. But this morning they let her play in Big Woods. That's because they went to the Airport in the City with my mom and dad. They went with some of the other people who live in Section A.

There's a spaceship coming in from Earth today. It's the first spaceship from Earth in a very long time. Whenever a ship flies here from Earth, all the grown-ups get very excited. Then they don't pay much attention to us kids.

They used to take us along to see the spaceship arrive and unload. They used to let us hear the news about Earth that the Spacers bring. But most of us kids would rather stay home. The Spacers always tell terrible stories about what's happening on Earth. Then the grown-ups just stand around looking awful, as if the bad news were their fault. Now they let us stay at home. They go to the Airport by themselves. There's nothing on *this* world that can harm anybody. So they never have to worry about our being alone.

Selena and I spent the whole morning in Big Woods. We found a lot of gingery snaps. The gingery snaps are a funny purple color, but they're really good to eat. Mom says that they taste a little like the mushrooms on Earth. But I don't know if that's so. I don't remember about mushrooms. I don't know if I ever ate any of them on Earth.

We came out of Big Woods with our buckets of gingery snaps. We walked across the meadow toward my house. As we went, we picked white and yellow flowers and put them in our hair. That made us feel beautiful.

Soon I saw my house. I saw that there was smoke coming out of the chimney.

"My mom and dad are home," I said to Selena. "Mom likes to make a fire in the fireplace, even if it's a warm day. She says it **reminds** her of the house she used to live in on Earth."

Selena said, "I guess my parents are home too. I better go and see what chores they have for me to do."

"Maybe they won't have any for you," I said. "You know how strange they always act after they've talked to the Spacers."

"That's right!" said Selena. "Maybe we can go wading later."

"And afterwards, we'll fly our kites."

"I'll bring mine when I see you later," said Selena. "Good-bye, Hope."

"Good-bye, Selena."

Selena hurried off to her house, and I walked through the meadow and across our little garden. Our house is exactly like all the other houses in Section A. They were built the same, one after another, when we got here. The house is made of logs and stone, and it has stone floors. I love the house. It's much nicer than the house we had on Earth, at least the way I remember our house on Earth.

When I came in, Mom and Dad were sitting at the big table in the middle of the room. They both looked up at me. I saw something shiny running down Mom's cheeks, and I knew that she had been crying again. I went over to her, feeling unhappy, as I always do whenever Mom cries.

"Hope, honey," she said, and hugged me tight. "Oh, honey."

"What is it, Mom? What's the matter?"

"It's nothing, dear."

She let me go and rubbed her eyes.

I looked at Dad and said, "Did you speak to the Spacers after they visited Earth?"

"Yes, Hope," he said. "We spoke to the Spacers."

I asked, "How come they were so late getting here this time?'

Dad's face was filled with pain that he couldn't hide. Dad said, "Things on Earth are very bad now, honey. Things on Earth are worse than ever."

"Will there be any more spaceships coming from Earth?"

Dad didn't answer for a long time. Then he finally said, "Probably not. There probably won't be any more ships coming from Earth."

"Well," I said. "That's not important, is it?"

Mom and Dad looked shocked and scared and sad, all together. But they didn't say anything. They just looked at me in that sad, strange way.

I knew that I'd said something wrong. But I didn't know what—not exactly. I said, "I better go and clean these gingery snaps for dinner. Selena and I picked them in Big Woods today."

"Yes," Dad said. "You do that, Hope."

I went into the kitchen and filled a big wooden bowl with some of the water Dad carries up from the stream every morning. I washed the gingery snaps and left them on the table, ready to be cooked. Then I went outside. But when I passed the window, I could hear Mom and Dad talking again.

Mom said, "Hope doesn't understand, John. She doesn't understand. She only knows 'it's so wonderful here.'"

"Maybe it's better that way," said Dad.

"I don't know. I don't know," said Mom. Her voice was getting higher and louder. "It's been more than seven years since we came here, John. But it seems like seventy! No, it *seems* more like seven hundred! *Seven hundred years of nothing to do!* Nothing to *do*. There's nothing to work for because it's already 'so wonderful here'!"

"Yes," said Dad. "Yes, Karen, I know."

Mom was crying again. "I wish we could go home," she said. "I wish we could go home!"

Mom was silent for a minute. Then she started to speak again. She spoke so softly that I could hardly hear her.

"Maybe we should *all* go home," she said. "Maybe we could change what we let happen to our world. Maybe we could make it wonderful *there* again too. At least we'd have something to work for."

"Karen," Dad said, "you know that we can't go back." Then Mom began to **sob** again.

I went away from the window and walked toward Selena's house. I don't like to listen to Mom cry. And it's worse because I really *don't* understand. I don't understand why they talk that way after they speak to the Spacers.

Earth is a terrible place. I was only four years old when we left, so I don't remember much about it. But I've seen the photos that the Spacers brought. It's just awful there. The trees and flowers and plants are all dead. There's no sunshine. It's thick gray all the time. And you can't breathe without putting a mask over your mouth and nose. That's why almost everyone has left to come to a world like this one. That's why *we* came.

I just don't understand Mom and Dad and all the other grown-ups. Why do they act as if they're homesick or something?

Why would anyone want to go back to a place like Earth? Why would anyone want to go back to Earth when it's so wonderful here?

## LOOKING FOR FACTS IN THE STORY.

How well can you find facts in a story? Put an *x* in the box next to the right answer.

1. All the houses in Section A were
   - ❑ a. alike.
   - ❑ b. different.
   - ❑ c. made of bricks.

2. Hope and her parents left Earth
   - ❑ a. more than seven years ago.
   - ❑ b. more than seventy years ago.
   - ❑ c. more than seven hundred years ago.

3. Dad said things on Earth were
   - ❑ a. better than ever.
   - ❑ b. worse than ever.
   - ❑ c. about the same.

4. Hope thought that Earth was
   - ❑ a. an exciting place.
   - ❑ b. a beautiful place.
   - ❑ c. a terrible place.

|  | x 5 = |  |
|---|---|---|
| **NUMBER CORRECT** |  | **YOUR SCORE** |

## EXAMINING VOCABULARY WORDS.

Here are four vocabulary questions. Put an *x* in the box next to the right answer. The vocabulary words are printed in **boldface** in the story. You may look back at the words before you answer the questions.

1. The cold water made her toes numb. The word *numb* means
   - ❑ a. dumb.
   - ❑ b. pleased.
   - ❑ c. not able to feel.

2. Her parents made her work. They gave her chores. The word *chores* means
   - ❑ a. jobs.
   - ❑ b. presents.
   - ❑ c. money.

3. The fireplace reminds Mom of her house back on Earth. The word *reminds* means
   - ❑ a. makes one remember.
   - ❑ b. helps one leave.
   - ❑ c. lets one enjoy.

4. The bad things on Earth made Mom sob. The word *sob* means
   - ❑ a. whisper.
   - ❑ b. laugh.
   - ❑ c. cry.

|  | x 5 = |  |
|---|---|---|
| **NUMBER CORRECT** |  | **YOUR SCORE** |

# A DDING WORDS TO A PARAGRAPH.

Complete the paragraph below. Fill in each blank with one of the words in the box. Each word appears in the story. There are five words and four blanks, so one word in the box will not be used.

Earth is about 93,000,000

_____ from the sun.
<sub>1</sub>

If _____ were too
<sub>2</sub>

close to the sun, we could not

live because of the heat. If Earth

were too far from the sun, we

could not live because of the

_____ . We are
<sub>3</sub>

lucky that Earth and the sun are

_____ where they are.
<sub>4</sub>

| scared | exactly | cold |
| Earth | miles | |

[ ] x 5 = [ ]

NUMBER       YOUR
CORRECT     SCORE

# R EADING BETWEEN THE LINES.

These questions will help you think critically. You will have to think about what happened in the story, and then figure out the answers. Put an *x* in the box next to the right answer.

1. We may infer (figure out) that Hope and her family live
   - [ ] a. on Earth.
   - [ ] b. 100 miles from Earth.
   - [ ] c. somewhere in space.

2. Which sentence is true?
   - [ ] a. Hope loved Earth.
   - [ ] b. Hope's parents cared very much about Earth.
   - [ ] c. Hope had no friends.

3. Hope was living in a place
   - [ ] a. that had no trees.
   - [ ] b. that had no sunshine.
   - [ ] c. that was very safe.

4. The writer seems to be saying that
   - [ ] a. we should take better care of Earth.
   - [ ] b. there are plenty of wonderful places to live.
   - [ ] c. children can have fun anywhere.

[ ] x 5 = [ ]

NUMBER       YOUR
CORRECT     SCORE

# NOTING STORY ELEMENTS.

Some story elements are **plot, character, setting,** and **mood.** Put an *x* in the box next to the right answer.

1. What happened first in the *plot*?
   - ❑ a. Hope and Selena spent the morning in Big Woods.
   - ❑ b. Hope cleaned the gingery snaps for dinner.
   - ❑ c. Hope heard Mom and Dad talking as she passed the window.

2. Which sentence *characterizes* Karen and John?
   - ❑ a. Their lives were exciting.
   - ❑ b. Their lives were not very interesting.
   - ❑ c. Their lives were filled with danger.

3. Who is the *main character* in the story?
   - ❑ a. Hope
   - ❑ b. Selena
   - ❑ c. Karen

4. When is the story *set*?
   - ❑ a. in the past
   - ❑ b. in the present
   - ❑ c. in the future

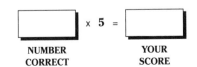

|  | x **5** = |  |
| --- | --- | --- |
| **NUMBER CORRECT** | | **YOUR SCORE** |

## THINKING MORE ABOUT THE STORY.

Your teacher might want you to write your answers.

- ◆ Do you think you would like to live where Hope lives now, or would you rather live on Earth? Explain.
- ◆ Why do Hope and her parents have such different feelings about Earth?
- ◆ There may not be any more spaceships coming from Earth. Explain why. What lesson or lessons does the story teach?

Use the boxes below to total your scores for the exercises. Then write your score on pages 138 and 139.

| | |
| --- | --- |
| ☐ | **L** OOKING FOR FACTS IN THE STORY |
| + | |
| ☐ | **E** XAMINING VOCABULARY WORDS |
| + | |
| ☐ | **A** DDING WORDS TO A PARAGRAPH |
| + | |
| ☐ | **R** EADING BETWEEN THE LINES |
| + | |
| ☐ | **N** OTING STORY ELEMENTS |
| ▼ | |
| ☐ | **SCORE TOTAL:** Story 12 |

# Acknowledgments

Acknowledgment is gratefully made to the following publishers, authors, and agents for permission to reprint these works. Adaptations and/or abridgments are by Burton Goodman.

"Uneasy Homecoming" by Will F. Jenkins. Reprinted by permission of the author's estate and its agents, Scott Meredith Literary Agency, L. P., 845 Third Avenue, New York, New York 10022.

"Mean Rocky" by George Shea. All attempts have been made to locate the copyright holder.

"His Best Time" by Elizabeth Van Steenwyk. Reprinted by permission of the author.

"The Attic Door" from *Tales for the Midnight Hour* by J. B. Stamper. Copyright © 1992 by J. B. Stamper. Reprinted by permission of Scholastic, Inc.

"The Cricket" from *The Day It Snowed Tortillas: Tales from Spanish New Mexico* retold by Joe Hayes. Reprinted by permission of Mariposa Printing & Publishing, Santa Fe, New Mexico.

"The Ghost of Wan Li Road" by Kara Dalkey. Reprinted by permission of the author.

"A Helping Hand" by Janet Ritchie. Copyright © 1986 by Jack Ritchie Estate. Reprinted by permission of Larry Sternig and Jack Byrne Literary Agency.

"It's So Wonderful Here" by Bill Pronzini. Reprinted by permission of Larry Sternig and Jack Byrne Literary Agency.

# Progress Chart

1. Write in your score for each exercise.
2. Write in your Score Total.

| | L | E | A | R | N | TOTAL SCORE |
|---|---|---|---|---|---|---|
| Story 1 | | | | | | |
| Story 2 | | | | | | |
| Story 3 | | | | | | |
| Story 4 | | | | | | |
| Story 5 | | | | | | |
| Story 6 | | | | | | |
| Story 7 | | | | | | |
| Story 8 | | | | | | |
| Story 9 | | | | | | |
| Story 10 | | | | | | |
| Story 11 | | | | | | |
| Story 12 | | | | | | |

# Progress Graph

1. Write your Score Total in the box under the number for each story.
2. Put an *x* along the line above each box to show your Score Total for that story.
3. Make a graph of your progress by drawing a line to connect the *x*'s.

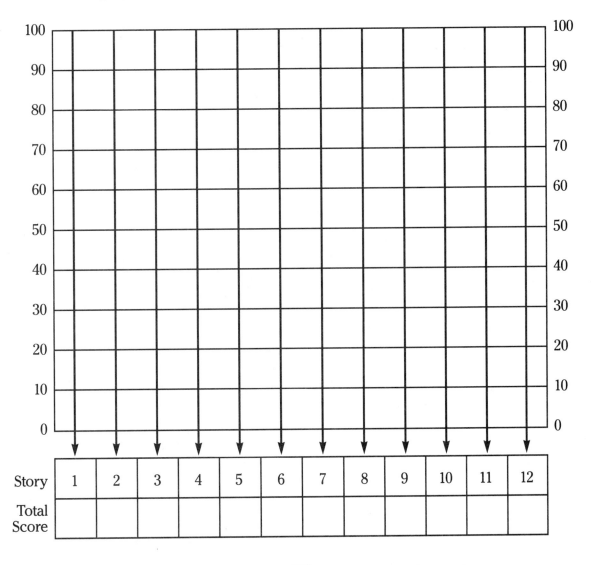